LIONS,
GURUS

LIONS, PRINCESSES, GURUS

Reaching your Sikh Neighbour

Ram Gidoomal and
Margaret Wardell

Highland Books

GODALMING
SURREY

First published in 1996 by Highland Books, 2 High
Pines, Knoll Road, Godalming, Surrey, GU7 2EP.

Cover Design by Paul Clowney

British Library Cataloguing-in-Publication Data. A
catalogue record for this book is available from the
BritishLibrary.
ISBN: 1 897913 35 4

Printed in Great Britain by Caledonian International
Book Manufacturing Limited, Glasgow.

CONTENTS

ACKNOWLEDGMENTS

When we thought of writing a book for Christians in Britain to help them reach out to Sikhs we first looked to see what was already available. Except for a small book written for Canadian Christians by Raj Santosh, we drew a complete blank. There are plenty of secular publications about Sikhism but nothing for the Christian man or woman who has Sikh neighbours and wants to share the love of Jesus with them. Here is our attempt to fill that gap.

Many people assisted in its production. We would especially like to thank those who read the first draft and made numerous helpful comments and suggestions. They include Alex Abraham, Julia Cameron, David Corfe, Rana Johal, Narinder Kang, Sunil Kapur, Sheila Kanwal, Narindar Mehat, Santosh Ninan, Sunil Raheja, Kuldip Rajo, Raj Santosh, Basil Scott, Graham Stockton and Hilary Warner. Special thanks go to Suk Gill for supplying the material for chapter 2.

Throughout the book people's names have been used to illustrate specific situations. The situations are real but the names have been changed.

PREFACE

In the last 40 years many people from the New Commonwealth have settled in Britain. The 1991 census shows some 1 million of these are from South Asia, meaning those who come from an Indian, Pakistani or Bangladeshi background. It includes those whose forbears emigrated early in this century from those countries to East Africa, mainly Kenya, Uganda and Tanzania, and have now re-emigrated to Britain, often for political reasons. Among them are about 400,000 Sikhs[1].

This book aims to help Christians learn about the culture and religion of the Sikhs and to suggest ways of witnessing to them. Maybe that is a project that leaves you with misgivings. You may be a denominational leader who wants to encourage such witnesses yet wonders how you will explain your activities when all local religious leaders meet together. Some of these will almost certainly question or even oppose what you are doing. May we share this word from the Revd. Gordon Fyles of Emmanuel church, Wimbledon, given to us privately?

> In what biblical sense do we conceive of God as Lord of history at this moment? He is the God who motivated white British missionaries to take the Good News of Jesus to the Indian subcontinent from the 18th century onwards. Local people heard and believed the Gospel and churches were

established. Now, at the end of the era of imperial British rule, considerable numbers of Asian people – through political and commercial considerations which seeem to have no religious strand within them – have arrived and will achieve significant numerical growth. We clearly see God's sovereignty in sending out missionaries and are comfortable with that, and even feel we should send more. But when God, the Lord of all history, acts sovereignly – and who else could arrange such a convoluted turn of history such as brought Asians and, indeed, West Indians here? – we are uncomfortable and feel threatened. Yet what if God, as the decline of Western Christianity accelerates, proposes to switch the focus for His purposes from white British churches to Black and Asian Christian groups? When Christ first came, the star rose *in the East* to announce His arrival.

Dare we also suggest (contrary to conventional missionary theory) that converted Asians may often be in a better position than Westerners to evangelise *British* people? CS Lewis in *Miracles* affirmed that pantheism was 'the permanent natural bent of the human mind'. Elements of the Asian worldview seem to be more in tune with the views on the meaning of life which are common to most people today. These include:

❑ A belief in some life-force (a spark of the divine, or Nature with a capital 'N') which underlies every living being and seems more plausible than both the doctrinaire gods of various scriptures and crass materialism.

❑ A strong presupposition that there is more than one path, and that each individual needs to find the one that is "right for him". Therefore all fundamentalist views (not just Christian ones) are suspect.

The witness of someone who has been convincingly converted out of such a plausible worldview may carry more weight than the story of a typical European. Most of the latter, even if they have gone through a time of rebellion, have always assumed uncritically that the Christian God and the Bible were the 'gold standard' of religion. As you will learn, Sikhs are particularly plausible in the West. They have rejected some of the controversial dimensions of Hindusim, such as caste. That's why if you ever hear a Sikh thinker (perhaps on *Thought for the Day*, an ecumenical religious slot on British radio), you should find him most reasonable.

And when in the book a converted Sikh says 'I lost my family and all I got in return was meetings', must you not admit that the Church in Britain would benefit from an influx of new Asian believers who can teach its members about family and hospitality?

Most towns in Britain have a few Sikh inhabitants; the large cities have thousands. Who will tell them of Jesus if not their Christian neighbours, school friends and work colleagues? We are sure you have chosen to read this book because you take that responsibility seriously. May it help you on the road to effective witnessing.

INTRODUCTION

The Sikhs come from a relatively small area of India, the Punjab in the North West. The name Punjab means 'the land of five rivers'. It stretches from snow-capped mountains in the north to fertile green valleys in the south. The climate is extreme: 115^0F in May, followed by heavy monsoon rains in July and August; in winter the temperature sometimes drops below freezing point.

Most of the Punjab is good farming land and so many Sikhs in Britain are from village backgrounds. But it also includes industrial cities such as Ludhiana, Amritsar, Chandigarh and Jullundur. The total population of the Punjab, according to the 1991 Indian census, was 20,190,795 of whom about 12 million were Sikhs. About a million Sikhs also live in Delhi, India's capital.

The Sikh religion is practised by about 19 million people worldwide[1]. Few Westerners know much about it. This is not surprising as the number of Sikhs is small compared with those of other religions and until the last 40 years, the majority lived in one small area of India. The word 'Sikh' comes from the Punjabi verb 'sikhna', 'to learn'. So a Sikh is a learner or disciple.

Map of the Punjab, showing the partition line
between India and Pakistan and its five rivers,
the Jhelum, Chenab, Ravi, Beas and Sutlej.

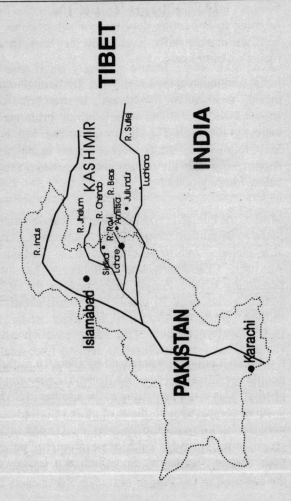

Three chief groups

Unlike Hinduism which divides itself into castes, the Sikh community is subdivided along professional or business lines. The Bhattras or traders were the first to come to Britain as door-to-door salesmen or to work on market stalls. Eventually they established their own businesses.

The Ramgharias are craftsmen, particularly carpenters. In India they were mainly townspeople. The British noticed their artisan skills and encouraged them to move to East Africa, especially Kenya and Uganda, in the 1890s, to help build roads and railways. When those countries became independent some Sikhs left to find their fortunes in the west. Others were expelled from Uganda by General Amin in 1972. But in the countries in which they have now settled they do all kinds of work. Some are doctors, lawyers, teachers, shopkeepers, nurses, factory workers. Most are interested in education. They still tend to marry among their own group and keep their own customs. In many places they have established their own gurdwaras (Sikh places of worship).

The Jats form the bulk of the Sikh population in the Punjab. They are agriculturalists, ranging from smallholders to powerful landlords. Most of them are sturdy, self-willed and industrious. They provide good military leaders and so are favourite recruits for the army. They are divided into various clans, each concentrated in groups of villages. The most important clans are Bains, Brars, Chahal, Dhillon, Gill, Randhawa, Sahota, Sandhu, Sidhu and Sindhu. Surnames are not used in the Punjab but when Sikhs came to

Britain they found they needed them for official purposes. Most adopted the name of their clan which explains why so many Sikhs in Britain have the same surname. Sometimes nicknames have become surnames e.g. Aikhani, the one who wears spectacles (ainakh means eye). The Jats are fiercely loyal to Sikh culture, though they do not always observe its spiritual teachings. Very few have become Christians and those who have have endured much persecution.

Whatever group Sikhs belong to, at critical moments they set aside their differences in the interests of the whole community. Thus persecution, and racial prejudice bind them more firmly together to face a common enemy.

The turban

To Westerners the outstanding mark of a Sikh man is his turban. But in fact not all Sikhs wear one; only those who have been initiated. They have taken a vow to cover their long hair and wear a turban in public, at all times. For someone to request its removal or, worse still, to knock it off, shows disrespect for the Sikh faith. It is not the same as asking someone to remove their hat. You are asking him to break a vow and lower himself in terms of religious integrity. Women who have been received into full membership are expected to cover their heads at all times.

News of opportunities abroad

Sikhs fought in the British army in both world wars. They formed about a third of the Indian army and nearly half their medal winners. As a result they learned of opportunities overseas. They were particularly interested in coming to Britain since it was the head of the Commonwealth. They also expected they would be well treated in Britain because they had proved their loyalty in time of war.

The first British gurdwara was established in Putney in 1911. But most Sikhs arrived here in the 50s and early 60s. In 1993 there were 180 gurdwaras in the U.K.[2] Some Sikhs went to the U.S.A and Canada, where there are about 200,000. Over 100,000 are in Vancouver in British Columbia. This is the second largest concentration of Sikhs in the world. Smaller numbers have gone to other countries; Australia and New Zealand, Europe, South East Asia and the Gulf. 8% of Sikhs now live outside India.

Thirty years ago some observers saw the Sikhs struggling to maintain their culture and identity and predicted they would be absorbed into Hinduism. But it has not happened that way. Today Sikhs throughout the world have a renewed sense of identity and Sikhism can take its place among the other worldwide religions.

Sikhs who came here mostly established themselves in cities where others from their own home village already lived. This was natural, as such people spoke the same language, practised the same customs and worshipped in the same way. However they tended to concentrate in relatively small areas, above all in Southall in West London, sometimes known as 'Little Punjab'. Other places where they live in considerable numbers are Gravesend in Kent and parts of the Midlands.

Why did Sikhs come to Britain?

Sometimes British people ask why they came. The answer is simple. They came because British firms invited them. In the days of full employment, in the 1950s, these firms placed advertisements in newspapers and on hoardings in India. For example, one rubber firm in Southall found itself short of workers. The assistant manager, who had served in the Indian army during the second world war said, 'The best soldiers we had were Sikhs. Why not send for some of them?' The firm found a few empty houses in one Southall street and sent for a couple of dozen Sikh men. They were happy to work long hours in an unpleasant atmosphere and pleased with their large pay packets.

But Sikhs are family men and wanted their loved ones with them. They wrote home saying, 'Our wages are good. We're going to stay. Come and join us.' And so whole families established themselves in Southall and other similar places. As the news spread through the Punjab that you could find employment and good money in Britain more and more Sikhs decided to emigrate. They naturally went to places where members of their family or home village were established and could help them to find houses and jobs. For instance, the core of the Sikh population in Southall comes from 12 villages around the city of Jullundur in the Punjab. Many of them came with hopes of making quick money and returning home but found that although wages were much higher than in the Punjab the cost of living was also higher, thus preventing them from saving enough to return to India.

Most resigned themselves to bringing up their children here, so a second generation of young people from a Sikh background are now growing up in Britain. They are British citizens by birth. Many have never visited the Punjab.

Christians who live in areas where there are Sikhs should be learning how to understand and relate to them. Above all they should be concerned to witness to them. Our previous book, *Chapatis for Tea*, has a chapter devoted to 'A Christian Response To Those of Other Faiths' If you want to witness to people of any other religion you would find it helpful to read it.

The *things to do* at the end of each chapter are crucial parts of the book. They suggest how you can act on what you learn. So take the book at your own pace. Read one chapter at a time and try to put into practice as many of the suggestions as you can. It would be ideal to do this in a group, studying one chapter a week at home, and then meeting to discuss the matters raised. Each member would follow up one suggestion and report back.

This book doesn't tell you everything about Sikhism. It is simply an attempt to present the basic facts which it is helpful to know when witnessing to Sikhs. As far as possible the book is non-academic (If you want to study the Sikh religion in more detail consult the book list at the back of the book). Part 1 sets the scene and gives guidelines for making Sikh friends. Part 2 explains the background of Sikhs and part 3 describes how to share the Christian message with them. In part 2, chapters three and four outline the history of Sikhism. Sikhs are very conscious of their history and studying it will help you to understand why they behave as they do today. Chapters five to 12 outline the basic beliefs and practices of Sikhism. Chapter 13 describes the ways in which Sikhs have adapted to life in Britain.

There is no standard spelling of many of the Sikh terms. We have resorted to the usual anglicised version and given their meanings in the glossary. To avoid the clumsy phrase 'he or she' one or the other sex is referred to in different chapters. Where your particular contact is of the opposite sex make the necessary mental adjustment.

You need to know something about the Sikh way of life to relate to them sympathetically, but you do not need to be an expert. Focus on ways of building bridges of friendship as you would with any new neighbour. However, you do not need to know intricate details of their beliefs and practices to be a friend nor, indeed, to witness to them. In fact, if you air your knowledge of Sikhism to Sikhs, in a 'know-it-all' manner, you will put them off – there is so much to learn that an inquiring attitude will yield surprises all the time. Instead, make sure you have a good knowledge of your own faith and can express it simply.

One matter of crucial importance is that Sikhs believe there are many ways to God. So talking will not persuade them that Jesus is unique. However, explaining the gospel is not doomed to failure; that would be to reckon without the Holy Spirit. He has the power to change hearts from within. Pray he will do so. The stories in this book of Sikhs who have come to Christ are powerful illustrations of that.

Most Sikhs are friendly, outgoing people and will welcome a chance to get to know you. Take courage. Make your first approach one of simple friendship and you may well build up warm relationships in which you can share your faith later.

Words explained in the glossary are in this font

Chapter 1

MAKING SIKH FRIENDS

Some years ago Jane was standing at a bus stop in London with an Asian friend. A white woman joined them and began to talk to Jane about some objectionable behaviour she had met with from someone who was an 'immigrant'. 'Were they West Indian or Asian?' Jane asked. 'Oh, I don't know,' the woman responded, and, pointing to Jane's Asian friend, 'one of yours anyway'. Somehow Jane managed to control her anger and refrain from slapping her.

Few people would be as crude as this woman. Nevertheless, many white people do have difficulty in recognising the individual characteristics of people who look as though they were born overseas. If we intend to share our faith with any of them we must see them as individuals and not just as part of a group who are all the same. If we make friends with Asian people we will soon discover that they are all different, just as people with white skins are.

How can I tell when an Asian person is a Sikh?

As we pointed out in the Introduction, some, but not all, Sikh men wear the turban. Most Sikh women wear the salwar kameez; long trousers, matching top, and thin scarf, or chunni. But some have adopted western dress. However the salwar kameez is not specifically a Sikh costume but, rather, Punjabi. East Punjab is a part of India, West Punjab part of Pakistan, so some ladies who wear this may be Pakistani and Muslim. Christian women from the Punjab will wear the same.

When you get to know Punjabis you may be able to tell whether or not they are Sikhs by their personal names. They do not have different ones for boys and girls. Surinder, Kuldeep, Harjit are among the common ones. If, after asking an Asian person's name, you are still not sure what religion she follows you should ask her. To a Westerner this may seem a personal question which a polite person would not ask but not to an Asian. She will be pleased to tell you as it shows you are interested in her. And it avoids your making a mistake which may upset her.

You should also be aware that many people who refer to themselves as Sindhi or Punjabi (indicating a place of origin) have some Sikh ancestry and may well combine both Hindu and Sikh practices.

Loving your neighbour

The basis of Christian friendship is loving our neighbours as ourselves (Luke 10:27), whatever their race, language or background.

The Christian interpretation of 'a neighbour' is anyone with whom we are in contact. Sikhs also believe they should love their neighbours though they would not express their belief in the same way. Sewa, service of their fellowmen, is a very important doctrine. When Amanda lived in London the Sikh family next door to her were always concerned about her welfare. She was often on the receiving end of their service, for meals, gifts and even a candle on an evening when the lights failed.

Many British people are not sure they want to be friends with people of a different racial background. They prefer to continue living in their own culture and behaving as they have always done. Jesus came to earth out of love for men and women. What a contrast life here must have been after heaven! Have you ever thought of him as the supreme example of a cross-cultural missionary? Christians need to imitate him in adapting to people of a different race. The only way to share the gospel with Sikhs is to get to know one or two of them on a personal level. These will usually be neighbours or work colleagues. Only public evangelists can share Christ with large numbers of people. Most of us do not have that gift or calling. But all of us can witness to one or two Asians whom we know well. This is much more effective than having superficial relationships with a large number.

Ways to get to know Sikh people

There are many such ways. Live in the same area, talk with them at work or over the garden fence, take your recreation in places where they do, meet Asian parents through the local school, volunteer to help Asians seeking to improve their English. If your corner shop is run by Sikhs, do at least some of your shopping there and linger to talk to the sales person or other customers.

When you have struck up an acquaintance with a Sikh you can ask her to teach you to say, 'Good morning' or 'Good afternoon' in Punjabi. But be careful to ask someone of your own sex. In Punjabi culture women do not talk to unrelated men casually. So if a white woman speaks to an Asian man he may think she is making a sexual advance. The same applies to white men approaching Asian women. At least early in a friendship, stick to conversations with your own sex (there can be exceptions with second-generation, westernised Sikhs).

This sort of conversation is merely an ice breaker. You have to develop a relationship of trust with people of any race before you can expect them to share deeper needs with you. So build up caring friendships.

Visiting a Sikh home

If you visit a Sikh home you may be nervous about how you ought to behave. Do as they do and you will avoid causing offence. In your home do not comment if Sikh guests act in unexpected ways. When you get to know them better you can talk about the differences between you and build up mutual understanding. Of course, if you have no language in common, it is more difficult. But even then you can express your friendship. Visit them if they are in trouble. Simply go and sit quietly with them. You do not need to show your sympathy in words. They will know why you have come. If appropriate, you could hold the hand of someone of the same sex to let them know you care.

Hospitality ranks high in Asian culture. Accepting invitations to the home of Sikh friends is the best way to get to know them. Always eat what is put before you even if you do not like it. In Asian society accepting the food a person offers is a sign of accepting them. Refusing it is hurtful.

The more time you can spend in a Sikh home, observing what they do, how they treat each other, the pictures on the walls, the TV and video programmes they like, the better you will be able to understand them.

Invite them to your home in return but do not be surprised if they do not come. They may be nervous about how they ought to behave. Do not stop going to them because of this. They will usually be delighted when you keep on coming. And when you really get to know them you will be able to share the gospel in a relaxed atmosphere.

Understanding someone's point of view

Do not just observe their customs and listen to what they say. Try to understand why they act and think as they do. This will take time. Asian people do not hurry visiting. They engage in general conversation as a prelude to talking about serious matters.

Issuing an invitation to an Asian family

Asian families are very close. If you invite them to a meal or to join you in an activity they will take it for granted that the whole family is included. They will appreciate your inviting their children to play with yours. You can also suggest taking part in a sporting activity or watching one. A few Sikhs are vegetarians but most do eat lamb and chicken. Never offer them beef or a dish cooked in beef fat or oil as this is taboo for most Sikhs. If you are unsure what they eat ask them when you issue the invitation. Punctuality is not so important in Asian culture as in British so Sikh friends may turn up later then you expect for something to which you have invited them. If they are coming for a meal save yourself worry by preparing food which does not have to be eaten as soon as it is cooked.

Some warnings

Be concerned about their needs.

Don't be so eager to share the gospel that you ignore other obvious needs. If you do they are unlikely to listen to what you say about your faith.

Remember that your Sikh friends are not objects to be done good to. Such an attitude is patronising and offensive. They are friends with whom you can share interests and heartaches. Do not do all the talking and giving. They too have much to give. Listen carefully when they tell you about their family, their background, their interests and so on. They are usually glad to introduce you to their language and culture. When you are in trouble confide in them. They have often suffered themselves and will usually be comforting and supportive. Always accept gifts or invitations they offer if you can.

Be careful about humour.

This is different in different cultures. You may unwittingly hurt people if you are not aware of this. The favourite British habit of leg pulling, in particular, is not understood as funny in Asian culture.

Realise they have problems

We should not be so occupied with our own problems that we fail to realise that our Sikh friends may have more serious ones than we do.

The older generation feel like aliens in a strange land and keep to their Asian culture as far as they possibly can. They need special help and prayer.

But Asian people under 30 have probably been born in Britain. Do not refer to India or East Africa as 'your country' when talking to them. They are British citizens and may never have visited the country of their parents' origin. At the same time they may not easily identify with British culture either. Such young people have a foot in two cultures; Punjabi at home and British at school or work. This can lead to uncertainty as to who they really are. Discussing the cultural tensions they experience can be a way of initiating conversation with them.

Friendships at work

These may develop through being involved in the same project, helping in a difficult job, or just sitting by a Sikh in the canteen. If you are in a position of authority do treat Asian workers just as you would someone British. If an Asian fails to do a job satisfactorily never imply that this is due to his colour, race or religion.

Whatever your situation remember that you are an ambassador for Jesus Christ. Treat Sikh people as you know He would treat them. You will not go far wrong if you observe this and pray regularly for your Sikh friends and contacts.

In Chapter 2 of *Chapatis for Tea* we went into some detail about making friends with Hindus. Much of it applies to making friends with Sikhs too. So we have only mentioned the main points here. If you want to get to know any Asian people we suggest you read the relevant chapter in the other book. In fact the whole of it would be good background reading, as witnessing to Sikhs has much in common with doing so to Hindus.

Things to do

1. Visit the local Asian corner shop if there is one and get to know the shopkeeper and his family. Ask them where they come from. Get them to tell you about their family background.

2. Think of other ways you could naturally meet Sikhs and build up friendships.

3. Make contact with local Asian Christians. The agencies listed on page 219 can help you. They can also help you get to know Sikhs in your area.

Chapter 2

SIKH CHARACTERISTICS

Here are the chief ones, which we feel that Sikhs themselves would mostly agree with:-

❑ Sikhs emphasise the family and reject asceticism. This has resulted in considerable social progress. Women are freer than in most Hindu areas of India. Many Sikhs value education for girls as well as for boys.

❑ They take their duty towards the community seriously, founding hospitals and orphanages and having a general sense of industry and responsibility. High class family members may be seen at their place of worship sweeping the ground, cleaning utensils and fetching water. A devout Sikh tithes.

❑ They are hospitable and will go out of their way to make a stranger feel welcome. They are polite and rarely turn away a person in need of help.

❑ They are loyal – intensely so on religious grounds. Many Sikhs have suffered martyrdom for their faith. They are especially loyal to fellow worshippers and friends.

❑ They are independent and democratic, all equal
  members of a brotherhood, the 'Khalsa', or pure
  ones. This spirit of independence has put a
  premium on organisational and military ability
  as they have constantly had to oppose
  domination by the Moghul emperors and later
  the British. They have always been a minority in
  the midst of unsympathetic majorities and are
  sensitive about domination by outsiders.

❑ They have a notable sense of humour despite
  their often tragic history. They love to make up
  jokes, even about themselves.

❑ They are fatalistic, having absorbed ideas of
  both Hindu karma and Muslim kismet. They
  believe in accepting whatever fate brings them.
  However, their opposition to asceticism saves
  them from the helplessness and apathy of
  extreme fatalism.

❑ They are adaptable and flexible. This seems to
  be linked to their fatalism. They will make the
  most of any circumstance and adjust accordingly
  since they consider what is happening to them as
  God's will. Their vigour of mind and body
  enables them to withstand the changes of a
  rigorous climate. Even persecution, the
  destruction of their homes and sacred buildings,
  and the enslavement of their women and
  children did not crush their spirit.

❑ They are often physically courageous. Their
  ancestry and history have bred in them a warrior
  strain. The later gurus developed the idea of the

soldier-saint which dominates Sikh attitudes to this day. They see themselves as forced, by a hostile religious and political environment, to fight for their existence as free men.

Of course, like people the world over, not all Sikhs exhibit all these characteristics. Some of them indeed have undesirable ones. They can be proud, unforgiving and a few are even violent. However, do not concentrate on negative qualities you may find in a few Sikhs. Most are trustworthy and reliable and make good friends.

Things to do

1. Write down the name of any Sikh you know and pray for him regularly.

2. If you have Sikh neighbours make friends with them. Take time to stop and chat.

3. When you have broken the ice with your Sikh neighbours, visit their home. After that invite them to your home for a cup of tea.

4. Ask a Sikh friend to teach you how to say, 'Good morning' and 'How are you?' in Punjabi.

Chapter 3

HISTORY - The Ten Gurus
1469 to 1708

Ask a Sikh about her faith and, before long, she is sure to mention the ten Gurus. Sikhs believe that God played an active part in their history and still does so today. They are proud to be part of this process.

Since the dawn of recorded history, pious Indians have consulted teachers whom they believe can tell them about God and help them to experience him for themselves. In North India in the 14th and 15th centuries a loose association of such teachers were known as sants or holy men. They shared a number of beliefs including the conviction that God is one, without form, but pervading everything. The way to know him better is to meditate on his name (nam) or truth (sat). They rejected idol worship and caste. Most of them wrote hymns in the vernacular for their followers. None claimed final authority or accepted worship but taught men and women to follow God alone. The first Sikh Guru, Nanak, is best understood in this context.

Guru Nanak (1469-1539)

Sikhs revere Guru Nanak more than any other Guru. He was brought up an orthodox Hindu, though, as

Traditional portayal
of Guru Nanak

Muslims also lived in the area, he learnt something about Islam too. By the time he reached his teens he was dissatisfied with formal Hinduism, with its emphasis on ritual. He began a religious search, consulting Hindu holy men and later Muslims too. However he did not find satisfactory answers to his questions.

He began rising before dawn to bathe in the river before meditating on the name of God. Gradually followers gathered round him. They met together in the evenings to sing praises to God, often late into the night. One day when he was 30 years old he failed to return from his dawn river bathe. His clothes were found nearby so people assumed he had drowned. But three days later he reappeared. When his followers asked what had happened he remained silent. But the next day he began to speak saying, 'There is no Hindu or Muslim. So whose path shall I follow? I will follow God's path'. He explained that he had been taken to the court of God and given a cup of amrit (nectar) to drink. As he drank he felt blessed by God. He was told to rejoice in God's name and teach others to do so.

This experience transformed Nanak's life. He became conscious that he had a mission to reveal God's name to the world. Shortly afterwards he uttered the Mool Mantra, which enshrines his concept of divinity. From this point on, stories about him describe him as Guru (one who proclaims enlightenment). The stories are called janam sakhis.

It is unlikely that Guru Nanak contemplated starting a new religion. He was eager to establish the truth of his message rather than found a community of followers. To this end he journeyed to the main centres of Hinduism and Islam in the Indian sub-continent, encouraging people to reject ritual and seek to experience the presence of God in their own lives.

At the age of 50 he ceased travelling and settled with his family in the village of Kartarpur, near Jullundur. Gradually a community grew up around him. Under his leadership it developed its own rituals and character. Until then religious literature was in Sanskrit, the classical language of India, but now Guru Nanak composed many hymns in the vernacular for his followers to sing and meditate on. These, along with the hymns of some of the sants, form the basis of the Sikh scriptures. He also taught the importance of working out one's faith in daily life, emphasising honesty and diligence. He worked to improve the status of women, too.

He received many visitors. Some of them donated the money to build a settlement, including his home, a place of worship and a hostel for those who came to him seeking for truth. This was the forerunner of the gurdwara.

When he died in 1539 he left 974 hymns, many written down and others committed to memory by his followers. He also left a disciplined community, living as householders, regarding work as a form of divine service, worshipping together and meditating on God's name daily. These characteristics still form the basis of Sikh life in the 20th century and give Sikhism its cohesion and uniqueness. Throughout his life Guru Nanak tried to direct his followers to his teaching and away from devotion to himself but, not surprisingly, many did worship him. His successors all struggled with the same problem.

Guru Angad 1504-1552 (Guru 1539-52)

Guru Nanak nominated Angad as his successor because he had found him humble and obedient. Guru Angad practised meditation and austerity and became famous for his generosity and wisdom. As Guru Nanak's teaching spread it was no longer possible for all Sikhs to live near the Guru's settlement. Guru Angad held the community together and maintained its spread and growth. He made a collection of hymns and wrote a biography of Guru Nanak, circulating copies to the scattered congregations. They helped to bind the Sikhs together and counteract the teachings of rival sects which were growing up.

Sanskrit was the religious language of Hinduism. Tradition says that Guru Angad invented the Gurmukhi script. The word Gurmukhi means 'from the mouth of the Guru'. This was a calculated step to demonstrate the separation of the new teaching from that of Hinduism.

Guru Amar Das 1479-1574 (Guru 1552-74)

Amar Das was a distant relative of Angad. He had never met Guru Nanak and recognised that the latter's teaching needed to be adapted to the changing membership of the Sikh community. But he did not compromise on the basic truths that Guru Nanak had established.

Amar Das emphasised the unity and equality of all men and expressed it in practical ways. He established the langar or free kitchen where anyone might eat as long as they did not observe any caste or social distinctions in doing so.

He pioneered work among women and strove for their emancipation. He spoke out against sathi, the Hindu custom whereby a widow was placed on her husband's funeral pyre and burned to death along with his body. In orthodox Hinduism a widow was not allowed to remarry and was subject to constant humiliation. Amar Das encouraged widows to remarry and gave them a respected position in society. He even appointed some women to preach.

He established the custom of Sikhs gathering together twice a year for Baisakhi, the spring festival, and Diwali, which takes place in the autumn (the latter being shared with the Hindus). No one could join the festivities until they had first eaten in the langar, thus demonstrating that they were Sikhs rather than Hindus. (Hindus may not eat with those of other castes.)

Guru Ram Das 1534-81 (Guru 1574-81)

Ram Das was the son-in-law of Amar Das. His name means 'slave of God'. He founded the city of Amritsar, meaning 'pool of nectar'. Being near the trade route from Delhi to Kabul it prospered quickly. The Guru declared that Baisakhi and Diwali should be celebrated there. It soon became the focal point of Sikhism and still is today.

Ram Das initiated certain social reforms which helped to weld the Sikhs into a conscious community, separate from Hinduism. Its members were distinguished by their adherence to a living guru and the exclusive use of the vernacular in congregational worship.

He encouraged Sikhs to marry in the presence of the Guru or his representative, composing a marriage hymn which is still part of the Sikh marriage service.

By the time of Ram Das's death the Sikh brotherhood numbered tens of thousands and was growing steadily.

Guru Arjan 1563-1606 (Guru 1581-1606)

Guru Arjan was the first Guru to be born a Sikh. He undertook missionary journeys throughout the Punjab. Soon not only the peasants but many powerful landowners, mainly Jats, joined the movement. The Jats were an unusually able group of people and it was they who later led the fight against the oppression of the Moghul Emperors. They form the major and most influential group in Sikhism even today.

Guru Arjan introduced a 10% tax on the income of all community members. He used this for a number of building projects. In 1589 he authorised the building of the Harmandir at Amritsar. This was to be the central place of worship for all Sikhs. It was a square building with a door in each side to show that it was open to people of all castes. It was built on a platform sunk lower than the surrounding area. The worshipper had to step down to enter, recognising that a relationship with God was attained by submission and humility. The other name given to the Harmandir was the Darbar Sahib, the Court of the Lord. In the nineteenth century the present Golden Temple was built on its site.

Throughout Guru Arjan's guruship his elder brother, Prithi Chand, was a constant thorn in the flesh. In the 16th century the Moghuls invaded India from the North-West and by Guru Arjan's time they controlled most of North India. They set up their court in Delhi. At first religious liberty prevailed throughout the empire. For most of Arjan's reign he and the then Moghul Emperor Akbar lived in mutual respect and confidence. Peace and harmony reigned in the Punjab. But towards the end of Guru Arjan's lifetime Prithi Chand and his followers managed to turn Akbar against Sikhism. Guru Arjan's death largely resulted from this intrigue.

While Guru Arjan was visiting other parts of the Punjab, Prithi Chand compiled a hymn collection, including some of his own compositions, and attempted to put it forward as the authentic scripture for all Sikhs. Guru Arjan promptly produced an authoritative collection. He added his own hymns together with those of his father and the first three gurus. It was completed in 1604 and known as the Ad or Adi Granth. In 1605 it was installed in the Harmandir. Guru Arjan initiated the custom of bowing before the Adi Granth as the word of God.

Guru Arjan's rule saw not just a negative rejection of Hinduism and Islam but the flowering of Sikhism as a distinct faith. It had its own central place of worship, a volume of scripture, its own ceremonies and a religious language, Gurmukhi. Small Sikh townships were growing up across the Punjab.

In 1605 the Emperor Akbar died. The Sikhs were accidentally involved in the power struggle between Akbar's son, Jehangir, and his grandson, Khusam. Jehangir gained the victory and suppressed his enemies with great cruelty. He ordered the arrest of Guru Arjan and the seizure of his property. Before leaving Amritsar for Lahore, Guru Arjan appointed his young son, Hargobind, to lead the Sikh community. In Lahore the Guru was imprisoned and then tortured. He was made to sit on a red hot iron plate while hot sand was poured over him. After three days he was allowed to get up and walk into the nearby river where he quickly drowned. From then on Sikhism had to fight for survival.

Guru Hargobind 1595-1645
(Guru 1606-1645)

It was in Hargobind's time that the concept of Sikhism as a military brotherhood began. His father Guru Arjan left a message, 'Let him be fully armed on his throne and maintain an army to the best of his ability'. Hargobind declared that the use of arms was an extension of giving to charity i.e. a way of protecting those who could not defend themselves. He saw himself not as a political rebel but as opposing the Moghul emperor's policy of destroying Sikh and Hindu places of worship and forcibly dissolving the marriages of Hindus to Muslim women.

Some Sikhs were concerned that, instead of composing hymns and sitting quietly in one place, Hargobind kept an army. Others saw him as a prince rather than a holy man. But his followers were devoted to him. He maintained that warfare should only be a last resort in the cause of justice. But he saw injustice on every hand and so his army was often involved in conflict.

His reign saw the evolution of a new type of Guru, a soldier saint, with the power of a secular prince as well as a spiritual leader. From this time forward the Sikhs were increasingly involved in political movements aimed at some degree of independence from the Moghuls.

Hargobind made three lasting contributions to Sikhism: he restored the places of worship, including the langars, common eating places, and refuges for the needy, many of which had fallen into neglect; he provided a pennant for his troops. This, the nishan sahib is still the flag of Sikhism and one is flown over every Sikh gurdwara; thirdly he introduced the use of a kettle drum for his troops. One is kept in each gurdwara to this day.

Guru Har Rai 1630-61 (Guru 1645-61)

During Hargobind's last years all of his sons, except the youngest, died.

The latter was quiet and withdrawn and seemed unsuitable to be a Guru so Har Rai, a grandson was chosen instead. He emphasised the importance of the Adi Granth and saw that one was kept in each gurdwara.

Guru Har Krishan 1656-64 (Guru 1661-64)

Har Krishan, just a child, was taken to Delhi by the Moghul emperor. There he died of smallpox but not before he had nominated his great uncle as his successor.

Guru Tegh Bahadur 1621-71
(Guru 1664-75)

Tegh Bahadur was that youngest son of Hargobind who had been passed over in earlier years. But he proved the man to meet the demands of the time. He countered harassment from the Moghuls with great strength of character. He wished to live a peaceful life seeing to the welfare of the needy but could rarely do so. He showed great courage in the battles against the Moghul forces but he was not really the person to carry on the political development of the guruship.

During his rule the Moghul Emperor, Aurangzeb, began a systematic process of Islamisation. He ordered the closing of Hindu schools and the demolition of temples. Where this was carried out he had mosques built on the sites. He taxed non-Muslims heavily and forced many of them to convert to Islam. But as his oppression grew so did the opposition.

Tegh Bahadur travelled around the Punjab rallying the Sikh community against the emperor. As a result Aurangzeb summoned him to his court and imprisoned him. When Tegh Bahadur steadfastly refused to become a Muslim the emperor had him executed.

Guru Gobind Singh 1666-1708
(Guru 1675-1708)

Tegh Bahadur was only able to resist the Moghuls on a limited scale but, before his son Gobind was very old, revolution was occurring in many parts of the Moghul Empire. Chaos enveloped North India. Guru Gobind raised an army which was capable of resisting the Moghuls.

He was a fine leader in both war and politics; highly educated, a skilled horseman and warrior, chivalrous and generous. Sikhs still look back to him as the perfect example of manhood. He is seen as the last and greatest Guru after Guru Nanak. The events of his guruship laid much of the foundation of present day Sikhism.

In 1699 Guru Gobind ordered the Sikhs to assemble as usual for Baisakhi. There he reminded them that they were living in dangerous times but that he planned a scheme for strength and unity which would demand supreme loyalty. He drew his sword and asked for men to come forward to give him their heads. At first no one responded. Eventually one man did so. Guru Gobind led him into his tent. In a few moments blood gushed from beneath the tent and the

Traditional portrait of
Guru Gobind Singh
from *Pavan is a Sikh,* published
by A & C Black

Guru came out alone with a blood stained sword. Four more men followed, though many others crept away. At last Guru Gobind went into the tent alone and returned leading all five men unharmed. Some Sikhs say he had raised them to life, others that the blood was that of a goat. But all agree on the example of fearless devotion which the five men showed to Guru Gobind and his ideas. The Guru then gave them amrit, sugar crystals dissolved in water, in an iron bowl. He stirred the mixture with a two edged sword and invited them to drink it. When they had done so he declared them the Panj Pyare, the beloved five. Then 13 more men were similarly initiated. This form of Sikh initiation is still used today. It is performed by five members of the gurdwara who are considered particularly devout and called the Panj Pyare.

Guru Gobind proclaimed a code of discipline. Tobacco, halal meat (from an animal slaughtered according to Muslim custom) and sex with Muslim women were to be avoided. Initiated Sikhs were to form a brotherhood called the Khalsa, the pure ones. Its members were to take the name Singh meaning "lion", so Guru Gobind became Guru Gobind Singh. Women were admitted to the Khalsa and were called Kaur which means 'princess'. The members of the Panj Pyare were to be each from different castes to symbolise the equality of every person. Members of the Khalsa were to be recognised by five symbols, uncut hair, a comb, a sword, a steel bangle and special shorts. Sikhs today still wear these and consider membership of the Khalsa to be the supreme outward mark of their faith. See chapter 9 for more details about this.

Guru Gobind Singh revised the Ad Granth and included in it 116 of his father's hymns but none of his own. However he did write many poems, often to rally his followers. In the early 18th century the latter collected them in the Dasam Granth, the book of the tenth Guru.

Throughout Guru Gobind's reign the Khalsa was involved in fighting the Moghuls. The Guru lost his mother and all his four sons. Two of them, still children, were bricked up in a wall and left to die. The others fell in battle. In 1708 Guru Gobind Singh himself received a fatal stab wound. Before he died he took five coins and a coconut and placed them before the Ad Granth. He stated that there would be no more human Gurus. Then Guru Gobind Singh proclaimed the Ad Granth as Guru and gave it the name Guru Granth Sahib – Sahib means 'Lord' and this personalises the Sikh holy book. He also declared a new concept of the Guru. It was not just the message contained in the book. The book itself was the spirit of the Guru. This spirit would be present wherever a member of the Khalsa deliberated and made decisions in the presence of the Guru Granth Sahib.

Guru Gobind Singh is highly revered by Sikhs. Only the founder Guru Nanak is more highly thought of. In most Sikh homes you will find paintings of one or both of them on the walls.

All of the Gurus were remarkable men and the survival and successful development of Sikhism must be attributed to them. In addition the Jats who were assimilated into Sikhism in the time of the fourth and fifth Gurus soon formed the majority of its members. They were warlike landowners, with a proud independent spirit, and may have stimulated Sikhism's military development. Many Sikhs today are Jats and have inherited something of this same spirit.

Things to do

1. Ask a Sikh friend to tell you some of the stories he knows about the Gurus.

2. If you know a Sikh family, ask them to tell you about the pictures of the Gurus in their home. Usually they will have one or more in their living room.

3. Ask a Sikh friend if any local gurdwara has an exhibition of Sikh history. If so ask him/her to take you to see it.

4. Ask a Sikh friend to read some of the Granth Sahib with you. Then you read him a few psalms and compare the two.

Chapter 4

HISTORY - 1708 TO
PRESENT DAY

Sikh worship and practice have altered somewhat since the death of Guru Gobind Singh in 1708. But none of the fundamentals have changed. Respect for the Guru Granth Sahib has been at the heart of the Sikh faith, even in periods when the strength of Sikhism has declined.

In 1710 the Moghul rulers decreed that all followers of Guru Nanak were to be killed. But this only strengthened the Sikhs' resolve to survive. For generations fighting was their way of life. The soldiers, with their wives and children, were continually on the move, from one refuge to another. Somehow they managed to maintain their opposition to the Moghuls and also observe the teaching of the Gurus. The sense of a common identity fostered by regular meetings for worship sustained them.

Gradually the power of the Moghuls began to decline. By 1765 the Sikhs were able to organise themselves into 12 military groups covering most of the Punjab. Each Baisakhi they met together at Amritsar.

Maharaja Ranjit Singh

During the armed struggle for survival many gurdwaras passed into the hands of Hindus. But in 1780 another inspired leader, Maharaja Ranjit Singh, was born. In 1799 at the age of only 19 he captured the large city of Lahore and made it his capital. He went on to establish the Punjab as an independent state. It remained so until the British added it to their empire in 1847. Ranjit Singh had the Golden Temple restored and many gurdwaras built. During his reign and ever since Sikhs have been free to practise their religion.

After his death in 1839 the number of Sikhs declined. Some lapsed back into Hinduism. Others became Christians. Of those who remained Sikhs many did not live up to the teaching of the Gurus. Few wore the five K's (see chapter 9). Many gurdwaras became Hindu temples, though the Hindu priests often continued reading the Guru Granth Sahib. But there were some who remained faithful; among them individuals with leadership qualities. Through them several reform groups came into being.

Nirankaris

This group, known at first as the Lodhiana Mission, was founded by Baba Dayal Das (1783-1854). As a young man he was shocked to find Sikhs being married by brahmin priests, using Hindu rites. The Guru Granth Sahib was nowhere in sight. He proclaimed the evil of this and the need to return to naming and wedding ceremonies based on the Sikh scriptures. He declared that those who called themselves Sikhs should take control of the gurdwaras and purge them of Hindu practices. During the reign of Ranjit Singh he met strong opposition. When the British took control of the Punjab, Christian missionaries started to come in. Soon the Arya Samaj, a Hindu reform movement[1] began to infiltrate.As a reaction against this a considerable number of Sikhs became Nirankaris.

Dayal Das was a deeply spiritual man, interested primarily in the devotional aspects of Sikhism. He believed that Sikhs should go back to the teaching of Guru Nanak and so rejected the institution of the Khalsa. Sikhism taught that salvation was obtained by meditating on God. Guru Nanak had sometimes used the name nirankar to describe God. And Dyal Das described Guru Nanak as 'Nanak nirank', the formless one. Thus his followers became known as Nirankaris.

Today Nirankaris meet for worship each morning. They bow before the Guru Granth Sahib which is read by one of their members. If a leader is present he gives an interpretation. They are most active in promoting strict adherence to the traditions of Sikhism.

Baba Dayal's most lasting contribution to Sikhism was his insistence that Sikhs should use the Anand marriage ceremony, introduced by Guru Ram Das. After Baba Dayal's death it was practised by the Nirankaris, as well as other Sikhs. But it only became legal by the Anand Marriage Act of 1909. This gave Sikhs the legal right to use their own form of marriage service. Only in 1925 did the Gurdwara Act establish their right to control their own gurdwaras.

Namdharis (Kichas)

Another Sikh leader of the resistance to Hindu practices was Baba Ram Singh. He found Sikhs taking drugs and alcohol, eating meat, having extravagant weddings and demanding costly dowries. All this he declared to be completely against Sikh principles. He even reminded Sikhs that Guru Nanak encouraged the remarriage of widows. He opposed the veiling of women, infanticide and child marriage and said that men and women should not sit separately in services. He encouraged meditation on the name of God and the use of a rosary in prayer.

During the British occupation of the Punjab, Namdharis acquired a political character. Some Kichas were involved in violence which resulted in riots; 66 of them were executed by the British and Ram Singh was exiled to Burma in 1872. The sect was not legally recognised by the government till 1922. After that they joined the orthodox Sikhs in their struggle for control of the gurdwaras.

In the meantime the Namdharis had acquired two characteristics. First they became conscious of themselves as part of the Indian independence movement. Secondly they came to believe that Guru Gobind Singh did not die in battle but became a recluse until he installed Baba Ram Singh as Guru. In 1862 Ram Singh was recognised by the Kichas as the 12th guru. They believe Guru Gobind Singh still lives today and will one day reappear. After Ram Singh's death his brother and then his nephew became Guru. In 1989 Jagjit Singh, a member of the same family was installed as the present guru. He has about 700,000 followers.

Most Namdharis are vegetarians. Baba Ram Singh was a Ramgharia and most of his followers are from this group. They can be recognised by the way they wear their turbans laid straight across the head.

Singh Sabha Movement

The Singh Sabha was formed at Amritsar in 1873 to counteract the threat from Christians and the Arya Samaj. Sabha means 'society'. The members aimed to restore Sikhism to its original purity, to promote education, and to publish books and periodicals on Sikhism. In 1892 they founded the Khalsa College in Amritsar where today many young Sikhs study. The movement sent its members out to the villages to recall the villagers to the pure faith. Where they found gurdwaras in the hands of Hindus they tried to have them restored to Sikhs. In 1901 they succeeded in removing the Hindu status from the Golden Temple. In 1920 they set up the Central Gurdwara Management Committee (the Shromani Gurdwara Paranbandak) to manage all Sikh shrines, though they only received the legal right to do this in 1925. Decision making is now usually left to the local congregation unless it is a major one for which there is no precedent. Then the custodians of the four most important gurdwaras meet to make it binding.

Akali Dal

Some Sikhs formed themselves into a voluntary brigade committed to defending gurdwaras to the death. They called themselves the Akali Dal, the army of immortals, and can be recognised by their navy blue turbans. In 1925 the British government declared them illegal but the passing of the Gurdwara Act in the same year put them in control of many gurdwaras and locally elected committees. The Akali Dal defined a Sikh as 'one who believes in the ten Gurus and the Guru Granth Sahib'. Eventually their interest became mainly political and since India became independent they have become a political party in the Punjab.

Radha Soami

This is really a sect of Hinduism but also has some characteristics of Sikhism. Some of its members are ex-Sikhs. Their 'Master' lives at Beas in the Punjab, which has become their headquarters. A fuller account of this sect will be found in the book, 'Chapatis for Tea'[2]. Many Sindhis established in Britain as well as Punjabis and even English folk follow this teaching.

Ravidassis

Though the Gurus denounced caste, Sikhism has never been completely free from it. Some Punjabis became Sikhs from an outcaste background and are still looked down upon by the others. The largest group are the Ravidassis. They built their own gurdwaras because they were not welcome in those belonging to orthodox Sikhs. They trace their origins back to Ravi Das, one of the 15th century north Indian holy men who inspired Guru Nanak.

Valmikis

The Valmikis are an outcaste, sweeper group. Unable to gain acceptance within the Sikh Panth they turned to the Ramayana, one of the Hindu holy books. Today they recognise Ram as their founder guru. The Ramayana is the focus of their worship though some use the Granth as well. Most of them no longer keep their hair long or wear turbans and their beliefs seem closer to Hinduism than Sikhism.

Specialist groups.

Over the years many specialist sub-sects of Sikhism have formed. Not all their members wear turbans. Remember, only those who have been baptised do so. They are known as amritdhari, those who are initiated. The uninitiated are known as the sahajdari. No one is barred from worship because they have not been initiated and do not wear the outward signs. They are only required to cover their heads, and remove their shoes for worship, and respect the Guru Granth Sahib. In Britain some gurdwaras insist that men and women who wish to be considered for the committee must be amritdhari.

Post Independence development

In 1947 when India and Pakistan became independent the Punjab was divided in half. The east became part of India, the west part of Pakistan. Most Sikhs preferred to be in India and 2 million moved there from the areas which had become part of Pakistan. The Indian central government recognised the distinctiveness of Sikhism. In 1962 universities were set up in three of the main cities of the Punjab. They began to produce books and journals about Sikhism.

Sikhs are usually astute and ready to seize opportunities for improving their social and material position. Many of them have emigrated to various parts of the world, especially since the second world war. They are found wherever there are opportunities to prosper. Because of this, they have become conscious of Sikhism as a world faith and, as well as expressing themselves in Punjabi, are now ready to do so in English too.

Demand for a Sikh Homeland

Since the 1970s, many Sikhs have been asking for greater recognition of their religion and changes in the provincial government tantamount to independence. Those prepared to use force found a leader in Jarnail Singh Bhindranwala. In the early 80s unrest grew and Bhindranwala was accused of organising violent opposition to the government and plotting its overthrow. He withdrew to the Golden Temple complex and made it his headquarters. Months of growing tension followed until in June 1984 the Indian army, under a Sikh officer, stormed the Temple, in what became known as Operation Blue Star. A two day battle followed. Bhindranwala and a number of his followers were killed. You can read more about this in Mark Tully's book, *No full stops in India.*

But this was not the end of the troubles. Most Sikhs were outraged at the desecration of their most holy shrine and saw themselves as partaking in the same suffering as Sikhs of earlier centuries. Violence followed all over the Punjab and the Indian government was unable to contain it. In October 1986 Mrs Gandhi, India's Prime Minister, who had ordered Operation Blue Star, was assassinated in Delhi by two of her own bodyguard, who were Sikhs. Riots followed in Delhi, and even abroad where there were large numbers of Sikhs. In India, many Sikhs and Hindus were killed or injured. A large number were arrested. Even this was not the end. Shooting and killing continued in the Punjab. Unrest still occurs, and the future of the Punjab remains uncertain.

Demand for Home Rule

Some Sikhs are campaigning for an independent country centred on the Punjab and to be called Khalistan. They can be identified by their saffron turbans. On the other hand, there are Sikh cabinet ministers, army officers and civil servants who are loyal to the Indian government and against the Sikh agitators. Many other Sikhs, including a good number overseas, are worried that the violence in the Punjab has given the world a tarnished image of Sikhism. Nevertheless some, while not supporting violence or the Khalistan movement for complete independence, would like to see the Sikhs in the Punjab having more control over their own affairs. Even though they have settled overseas, most Sikhs in Britain are concerned about the fate of the Punjab. The majority have relatives there and worry about their safety. It is good to be aware of this when talking to Sikh friends.

The Healthy, Happy, Holy Organisation (3HO movement)

Sikhism is not a missionary faith as it believes that all ways lead to God. However in 1969 Harbhajan Singh Puri, a Sikh, founded the 3HO movement in the U.S.A., for Westerners who wanted to follow Sikhism. It was incorporated as a tax-exempt organisation not overtly tied to Sikhism. It grew rapidly and by 1975 had over 110 centres and 250,000 members. Most of these were young, white, middle class Americans and Canadians. They did not regard themselves as Sikhs but as 'yogis' and 'yoginis'. Most Punjabi Sikhs in America do not identify with them. One Sikh author described them as a 'tantric yoga cult' and was critical of their deviation from mainstream Sikh practice.

Things to do

1. Try cooking some Asian foods. Ask a Sikh friend or neighbour to come and give you some tips. She may also help you shop for the ingredients.

2. Visit a local Asian restaurant and sample some of the food. You will then have something to talk about when you next visit Sikh friends.

3. Try to have a few Asian knick-knacks around your home. It will make it seem more friendly to Asians you invite in. Before doing so check that the articles do not have any unsuitable religious or cultural significance.

4. Invite Sikh friends to join you in watching a video, visiting a museum or going on an outing.

Chapter 5

THE SIKH SCRIPTURES

The Ad or Adi Granth

By the time of Guru Arjan the Sikhs had a line of Gurus, a script (Gurmukhi), an organised community, a capital at Amritsar with a central shrine but no written statement of their beliefs. Only the elderly had any personal memory of Guru Nanak and his teaching. Sectarian groups were beginning to compile spurious hymns either to promote their own claim to be the true Sikhs or to bring the Guru into disrepute. Some of the earlier hymns had been passed on by word of mouth. Unless they were written down they would be lost. The Sikhs also needed a book which would summarise their religious beliefs and prevent them from falling into error.

Guru Amar Das had already collected the writings of Guru Nanak and some of his predecessors. In 1604 Guru Arjan used these and other hymns to form the Ad Granth. It became the authoritative scripture for all orthodox Sikhs. The word Ad or Adi means first, not only in time but also in importance. 'Granth' means anthology or book.

Guru Arjan gathered the best available manuscripts, simplifying the language of some of them. He aimed to produce a book which would inspire faith and also help the devotee to lead a balanced and wholesome life. No other collection of Sikh writings has matched Guru Arjan's Ad Granth. Sikhs and western scholars both believe that the original is still in existence at Kartarpur where Guru Nanak spent his later years.

Guru Granth Sahib

Guru Gobind Singh added to the Ad Granth some of the hymns of his father, Tegh Bahadur. On his deathbed Gobind called for a copy of the Ad Granth and told his followers that from then on there would be no human Guru. You will find an account of what happened on page 45.

An interesting feature of the Guru Granth Sahib is the inclusion of the writings of Hindu and Muslim holy men. Some of them are represented by only a verse or two, others by quite a large number. The most important are those of Kabir, a weaver, over 1,000 verses, and Ravi Das, an outcaste leather worker (cf page 53).

The Granth has 31 parts called ragas suited to various moods; morning, evening, joy, grief and so on. They are set to music and each part is named after its musical setting.

The first 14 pages contain the Japji. This is the most important part of the Granth and should be used in daily meditation.

Its opening lines, the Mool Mantra, were Guru Nanak's first poetic utterance, and are a summary of Sikh beliefs.

❑ There is one God

❑ Eternal truth is his name

❑ Creator of all things and the all pervading spirit

❑ Fearless and without hatred

❑ Timeless and formless

❑ Beyond birth and death

❑ Self-enlightened

❑ By the grace of the Guru he is known.

The Japji is the only part of the Granth never to have been set to music. Sikhs consider it the greatest aid of all to meditation. Many rise early, have a bath and then meditate on the Japji in order to fix God in the forefront of their minds before the busyness of the day. Other parts of the Granth are used for various purposes. The rahiras for evening prayer, the kirtan sohilla for funerals. The last 78 pages consist of hymns so short that they could not be placed in the main body of the text.

For nearly four hundred years printing of the Guru Granth Sahib was forbidden. Every copy was handwritten. This was a long and expensive process so whole villages had no copy. But the entire book, including pages and page numbers was printed and standardised in the late 19th century. Copies of the Granth are identical, anywhere in the world. Each has 1430 pages. There are 5,900 hymns in all. Some are very short, others several pages long. Each of the 31 parts contains the hymns of the Gurus in order of succession, then those of other holy men. The number of contributors varies from part to part. The largest contributor was Guru Arjan. 2218 of the hymns are by him, 974 by Guru Nanak, 907 by Guru Amar Das.

Contents of the Granth

In general, the poetry of the Granth resembles that of the Psalms and Proverbs, and the Song of Solomon. There is no historical narrative or logical prose teaching as in the New Testament. Nor any mythological stories as in the Hindu holy books. Certain ideas emerge by virtue of much repetition. Much of the Granth reminds one of the bhakti (loving devotion) school of Hinduism. God is seen as loving and personal. He offers salvation to those who faithfully meditate on his name. Prayers, both private and in the congregation, must be addressed to him alone. Hindu religious practices, such as the brahmin priesthood, pilgrimages, asceticism and above all idol worship, are firmly rejected.

However God is mentioned by many of the names used in Hinduism and Islam. There is even a reference to Jesus. And it is more than a mention of his name. His message and purpose are made clear.

God has destroyed the head of the Devil through
Jesus of the world.
There was a light in the heaven;
All came to congratulate Him,
blessed be the king of all people
The destroyer of the wicked
and Saviour of the poor;
The creator of the Universe

> Save me, I am your servant.
> God is one; may victory belong to Him.

Padshahi 10 Chaupai, Rahiras Sahib
quoted in Sundar Ghutka pp.299-300

The Granth declares that right living is essential to a proper relationship with God, so it is full of references to a person's conduct. It gives its readers guidance on how to live good and useful lives. The world, it says, is so full of temptations that it is difficult for the average person to keep his character free from blemish. Therefore all Sikhs should marry so that the family can support each other in trying to remain pure. Every able-bodied person should work for a living and share the fruits of their labour with the needy. Discrimination of all sorts, whether racial, religious, sexual or social is condemned.

No faith should be placed in other books claiming to be scripture, though the writings of other religions may be studied and insights gained from them. The words of devout men and women of today may also be read with profit. Such people have meditated on God and been enlightened by him.

Phrases and sayings from the Granth embellish Punjabi language and literature. Much of the teaching and hymns have become popular proverbs.

The complete Guru Granth Sahib is regarded as the gurbani, the total expression of the voice of God. It is difficult, even for those who regard their scriptures as inspired by God, to appreciate the intensity of feeling among Sikhs for the Guru Granth Sahib. Whereas in Christianity the ideal is for the Bible to be found in every Christian home, it is unusual for the complete

Guru Granth Sahib to be found in a Sikh home. Books for private devotion will contain selections from it but the ritual associated with the Sikh scriptures could not be carried out in the average household, so it is not found there.

The Guru Granth Sahib is written in Gurmukhi. This word is used for the script but the spoken language is known as Punjabi. Unfortunately the vocabulary of the Granth is very different from the Punjabi Sikhs use today. It is written in several different dialects and most Sikhs find it difficult to understand. Newspapers, books and other printed material for Sikhs are all written in more up-to-date Punjabi.

The Granth is normally sung and this singing of scripture is called the kirtan. The music is simple and straightforward so that the worshippers can join in. Usually three musicians take part. They use a drum, a portable harmonium, the result of British influence in the 18th and 19th centuries, and a lead singer. The singer often explains the text and plays an instrument too.

The Dasam Granth

Guru Gobind Singh was a great poet but he included none of his own hymns in the Granth. He did not want his writings to rival those of his predecessors. At the time of his death they were scattered in various parts of India. But a faithful follower gathered them together and published them in 1734. They became known as the Dasam Granth of the Tenth Guru. The Dasam Granth contains not only the works of Guru Gobind Singh but contributions from other poets who were in sympathy with his cause. The most important part is the Jap, reminding one of the Japji of Guru Nanak. It opens with the following statement about God.

> God has no marks or symbols
> He is of no colour, of no caste
> He is not even of any lineage
> His form, shape, size and garb
> cannot be described by anyone
> He is immovably self-existent
> He shines in His splendour
> No one can measure his might.

The Jap and some other verses are used in the initiation ceremony which is described in chapter 9. It is found in the small hymn book, gutka, that many Sikhs use for daily meditation.

However the Dasam Granth is not generally accepted as Scripture in the way the Guru Granth Sahib is. It contains 2,000 poems in 12 sections. All printed copies are identical and have 1,428 pages. The most spiritual poems occupy about 160 pages. The rest sometimes use secular language. A recurring theme is the challenge to Sikhs to stand up and be counted. It helped to develop the fierce independence of the Sikhs and their determination to survive against all opposition. Some parts are openly militant.

Things to do

1. Ask a Sikh friend how he prays and when he does so.

2. Try to get hold of at least the Japji and read it.

3. Ask a Sikh friend how he tries to put the scriptures he reads into practice.

4. Ask a Sikh friend to take you to a gurdwara to hear the singing of the kirtan.

Chapter 6

BELIEFS AND RELIGIOUS
TEACHING

Sikhism began in a largely Hindu environment. Much of the Gurus' teaching was an attempt to show their followers the shortcomings of Hinduism and to replace them with teachings they believed to be the truth. If you do not know much about Hinduism you may like to read 'Chapatis for Tea'[1] in order to understand the background out of which the Sikh faith developed.

Some Sikh concepts are abstract and may be hard to grasp but others are practical and down to earth. What follows is just an outline. If you want to know more details consult the book list at the back of the book.

Concept of God

Sikhs believe in one God. He is truth, he is eternal and self-existent. He is the creator of the universe. Its existence and survival depend on him. But he does not sit apart from it. God is in everything and everything is in him. He cannot be known or understood because his greatness is beyond comprehension. He is without qualities; yet men can experience, worship and love him. They can address him in personal terms. The scriptures emphasise that he is unknowable yet makes himself known in his Shabad (word), Nam (personality and character) and as Guru (one who is enlightened). This may seem contradictory to a western mind but an Asian has little difficulty in accepting it.

Sikhs refer to him as Sat Guru or Guru of Gurus. 'Gu' means darkness and 'ru' light or revelation. So the Guru dispels the darkness of ignorance and reveals true understanding. In the Sikh scriptures the word 'Guru' usually refers to God, not to the ten human Gurus. But he can be addressed in any manner so long as the term used means 'one almighty God' and not any human being or worldly object. The Jap of the Dasam Granth contains 950 names and adjectives for God. The Ten Gurus preferred to use the name Satnam, as in the Mool Mantra.

Sikhs reject the idea that God ever assumes physical form. Guru Arjan said, ' May the mouth burn by which it is said that the Lord becomes incarnate. He neither comes nor departs from this earth.' (Guru Granth Sahib 1136). Bowing to idols is also forbidden.

Sikhism also teaches the moral purity of God. This is in contrast to the Hindu gods who may be vindictive, deceitful and sexually immoral.

Concept of Humanity

Man is the crown of creation. He draws his life from God. The soul does not die and cannot be destroyed even by death. The body and soul cannot do without one another; they are complementary. God has given men understanding and the ability to reason. He has made them moral, value-conscious beings. However under the pressure of outside influences such as heredity, environment, bad habits or bad friends their judgment may be impaired and the voice of conscience go unheeded. Thus men can fall into evil ways.

All men are not evil by worldly standards. Many, in the course of their daily life, do valuable work for others besides themselves. But they are, nevertheless, ignorant of their true nature and destiny. Thus they live as if this life were the only one. Yet God has not left them without hope. He has given them his Word (shabad) and spiritual teachers to open their eyes to his eternal truths.

Spiritual teachers (Gurus)

Some confusion exists about the term Guru. Nanak used it to refer to God himself and it often still has this meaning. But it is also used of human beings in whom the spirit of God is revealed. Sikhs believe that the spirit of God was present in Guru Nanak and passed on from him into all the other nine Gurus. They were the mouthpiece of God and showed the way to him. Today that mouthpiece is invested in the holy Scripture, hence its name the Guru Granth Sahib.

The Sikh community as a whole is called the Panth. Some Sikhs say that it is another manifestation of the Guru. They believe that Guru Gobind Singh gave it that authority. This theory proved inconvenient in practice and the idea was dropped until recently. But nowadays, when it is popular to talk about democracy, the idea is sometimes revived.

Some Sikhs, particularly those belonging to the sects, believe there are living gurus today. The orthodox Sikh would deny this. But they do respect spiritual teachers. When such people are absorbed in contemplating God they believe they receive revelation about the problems of life. Spiritual teachers are not just passive channels of divine revelation but God's representatives in dealing with physical and spiritual problems. At crucial moments God's Word is revealed to them so that they can speak it out for the enlightenment of their followers. For instance Radha Soamis make pilgrimages to Beas, in the Punjab, where their present-day guru lives. He sees each of them individually and gives them a special word to help them live a virtuous life.

Reincarnation (samsara)

The soul goes through a continuous round of births and deaths. It may be reincarnated as any form of life. Guru Nanak says in the Guru Granth Sahib, 'We inhabited several plants and trees and were then reincarnated as animals. We were born as serpents of several species and then winged birds.'

Human birth is the best of all. Only man can distinguish right from wrong. Only man can hear the voice of God. By responding to this repeatedly he can reach a state of permanent bliss in God's presence; there is no more coming and going.

The Gurus taught that there are 8,400,000 rebirths. But every person does not have to go through all of them; the number can be modified by God's grace. The number or sequence of the rebirths was of little interest to the Gurus. Their message was simply that being born as a human being gives the soul a unique opportunity to know God. This is what men should strive for.

Works (karma)

Sikhism teaches that man is unique in creation because he can reason and enter into a voluntary love relationship with God. However he is attached to worldly values, a condition known as manmukh. Until he relinquishes this and is filled with God he will be repeatedly reborn. The position in which he finds himself, according to the law of karma, is a consequence of his actions in his previous life. His aim should be to achieve freedom from the round of births and deaths. He does this by becoming aware of the inner presence of God as Shabad, Guru and Nam to the point where he is completely under their influence. He is then known as a gurmukh, one who has attained union with God. It is only possible because God looks kindly on man's efforts to experience him and sets him free. But man is still responsible for his own right conduct. Unlike Hinduism the mark of the gurmukh is not renunciation of the world. The world is part of the one reality in which all exist. The gurmukh is to live out his freedom in it, not separated from it.

Karma is not absolute or inevitable in its effects. It can be modified by the grace of the God. But a Sikh can never be sure that God will be gracious. A devout Sikh tries to abide by God's commands and hopes he will be gracious. Whether he is or not is entirely in God's will.

Salvation (moksha)

Most men look to teachers to show them the way of salvation. While a human guru is not essential, the help and guidance of a gurmukh (God-conscious) person makes it easier for a man or woman to understand more about God. But a guru is only a guide. The initiative rests with the individual. He has to work out his own salvation through meditating on God's shabad and nam. To do so he passes through five stages on his way to perfection. Those who reach the final one are said to have achieved union with God; their actions are totally at one with God's will. At this point the law of karma is superseded so that the round of births and deaths ceases. Hindus believe such a state is achieved through yoga but the Gurus denounced such practices and said that meditation on God as Shabad, Nam and Guru is the right way. However someone who had turned from the Gurus to Jesus Christ said that no one knows of any Sikh who has achieved the union with God for which they long.

Meditation (nam simran)

This should be practised daily, not just once a week. The individual should attempt to concentrate his thoughts on God's name (nam). This is known as nam simran. It is not the mechanical repetition of certain syllables, as in the mantras of Hinduism, but reflection and concentration on the nature of God (nam). If he does this daily he will remember to be truthful in thought, word and deed. Constant remembrance of God is also the way to personal spiritual peace. 'A mind fixed on God becomes godly, on evil becomes evil'[2]

Prayer

Men and women should seek God's blessing on all their activities; moving into a new house, going on a long journey, starting a business and so on. But prayer does not reduce their responsibility to work or try to solve their problems themselves. They can ask God for help and guidance with their difficulties but not sit back and expect him to sort them out. They must do this themselves, with his aid. People may pray in their own words but the recitation of set prayers is also important. These help them to concentrate and fix their minds on God. Prayer disciplines men's emotions, enables them to obey God and leads them into truth.

Delusion (maya)

In Hinduism maya is described as 'illusion' but in Sikhism the meaning is rather different. It is 'delusion' or attachment to the world. It can be anything which keeps men from truth and union with God. It not only includes such evil traits as lust, greed, pride and anger but also love of the family or service of the gurdwara if these become ends in themselves. Attachment to maya must be replaced by attachment to God.

The Grace of God (nadar)

In Sikhism grace describes the way God focuses attention on a person. It has a number of meanings: he accepts and blesses a person: he sets a follower free from the struggle to win appreciation for his actions:

he transforms these into acts of service and free will: he reveals the meaning of life to those who seek him and gives them a sense of his presence. He does all this through his grace.

There is an element of fatality too about God's grace in Sikhism. We are good or bad in accordance with God's grace. We only understand if he chooses that we should. We cannot win grace by trying hard to do so. Only God can bestow or withhold grace. Only through his grace can we receive salvation.

God's will

In Sikhism there is no place for free will. Everything that happens is predetermined and occurs because God wills it to happen. But this is not the complete story. Right living will not spare a Sikh repeated rebirths but it can give him a better life in the next round.

Suffering

Suffering is God's will. Men have to reconcile themselves to it and submit willingly and cheerfully. Most suffering comes from self-centredness and attachment to material things. The way to wean oneself away from these is sewa, selfless service, and nam simran, the remembrance of God.

Sewa (Service to Others)

A God-centred life is to be lived in the midst of normal worldly activities. The enlightened should help those lagging behind on the road to spirituality, not cut themselves off by becoming absorbed in their own spiritual progress. Service of others can transform a person's moral and spiritual life. Practical service to the community is also important. People who serve should concentrate on the act of serving and not on its outcome.

Miracles

Some Sikhs may tell you of miracles the Gurus and other saints are supposed to have done. A few worship spirits contrary to orthodox Sikh teaching. Sikhs are warned that miracles and occult powers are useless and fruitless because they lead one away from God. No miracle is considered greater than just remembering God as often as one can during the day.

When Guru Tegh Bahadur was arrested he was asked to show miracles to prove he had God's authority to be the Sikh leader. But he simply repeated a hymn of Guru Ram Das:

> The desire to perform miracles is worldly
> and creates ego
> It is an obstacle in the way of repeating
> the Lord's name
> that resides in my heart.

Then he stood quietly waiting while the representatives of the Moghul emperor moved forward to behead him.

Things to do

1. How do Sikh and Christian beliefs differ? Find Bible verses which explain the Christian beliefs.

2. Ask a Sikh friend a) What she believes about God. b) What she believes about reincarnation. c) How she tries to put sewa into practice.

3. Ask a Sikh friend to tell you how she worships God. Then try to describe your own practice to her. Don't argue. Just exchange information.

Chapter 7

THE GURDWARA

Guru Hargobind was the first to use the term gurdwara for a Sikh place of worship. It means 'the abode of the Guru'. He visited places associated with his predecessors, restored the buildings and encouraged local leaders to use them for giving proper teaching to the local Sikh community. Today there are gurdwaras in every place where Sikhs live in any number. They may be ornate and purpose built or plain like any other building. In Britain a gurdwara may be a house or former factory. In Southall one gurdwara is a former dairy, one a former church and another a terraced house enlarged and extended over the years. Only a building in which there is a copy of the Guru Granth Sahib can be called a gurdwara.

Sikhs do not ask for outside help in building or adapting a building for use as a gurdwara as begging is forbidden. Service or sewa is highly esteemed and Sikhs usually give very generously to community projects. In one gurdwara in London the offering amounts to about £8,000 a week. Those who cannot afford to give money offer their skills and time. In most gurdwaras the leader will challenge the congregation to commitment.

Figure 7.1 The Sikh Flag
Taken from W. Owen Cole, Sikhism published by
Lutterworths Educational

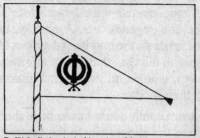

The Sikh flag flies from the top of the gurdwara all the time.

The Sikh flag, the Nishan Sahib, flies over every gurdwara or from a flag pole beside it. It is triangular, yellow in colour and the pointed end is finished with a tassel. It stays at full mast throughout the year. The flag pole is wrapped in cloth similar to the flag.

In the centre of the flag are three swords which form a black sign known as the khanda. The upright, two-edged sword in the centre represents freedom and justice. The curved sword on the right marks guidance in spiritual matters and the one on the left guidance in worldly matters. The circle in the middle, known as the chakkar, emphasises the balance between these two.

Before entering a gurdwara many Sikhs bow to the nishan sahib and touch the base of the flag pole with their foreheads if it is at ground level. Every Baisakhi (spring festival) the old flag is discarded and a new one installed in its place.

The Prayer room

This is the most important room in any gurdwara. Pictures of incidents in the lives of Gurus hang on the walls, but they are not worshipped. The floor is carpeted and covered with large white sheets on which the congregation sits. A narrow, uncovered strip of carpet down the middle of the room leads from the entrance to the Granth Sahib. Men sit on one side of the room, women on the other. Children usually stay with their mothers.

The Guru Granth Sahib has to be higher than the place where the people sit. In the centre front is a platform above which is a richly decorated wooden or silk canopy called a chanani. If it is silk it is usually heavily gathered and finished with a fringe. A large cushion, the manji sahib, is placed on the platform and covered with a soft quilt. Over this two white cloths are placed. On top of these are three small cushions. The Granth Sahib rests on these and is covered with a cloth, the rumala, as a token of respect. A rumala may be finished with a trimming. From time to time members of the sangat donate a new one. The space in front of the manji sahib is covered with a rug and decorated with fresh flowers.

A chaur, a sort of fly whisk, is kept beside the Granth Sahib. It is made of yak hair with a wooden or silver handle. When someone is reading they wave the chaur from side to side over the Granth Sahib at the same time. This is a sign of respect.

When people come into the gurdwara they remove their shoes and cover their heads. They walk down the centre strip of carpet to the Granth Sahib and place

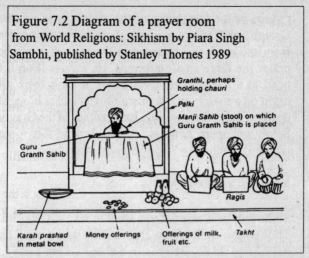

Figure 7.2 Diagram of a prayer room
from World Religions: Sikhism by Piara Singh
Sambhi, published by Stanley Thornes 1989

offerings of food and money on the rug. Then they
kneel and touch the floor with their foreheads. The
offerings are used for the maintenance of the gurdwara and for helping any needy person. Food is taken
to the kitchen. Giving an offering is not compulsory
but a matter between the individual and God (p. 113).

After the service each member of the congregation
is given a little kara prasad to eat (p. 87). As they do
so they bow and speak a few words of praise to God.
Then they go to the dining room, where they share a
meal. Both this and the room are called the langar.
Shoes are not worn here and heads remain covered.
Different families usually pay for and prepare and
serve the meal. To do so is considered one of the
greatest acts of charity a Sikh family can perform.
Everybody is expected to eat the same food as a
symbol of unity and equality among Sikhs.

One of the last duties of the granthi is to put the Granth Sahib to rest at night. He removes the rumala from the book and wraps it in the two white cloths under the three small cushions. He carries it on his head to a room above the canopy. It stays there all night on a manji sahib under a rumala and is brought down again in the morning. Extra copies of the Granth Sahib and spare rumalas are also kept in this room which is reached by steps from the main room.

Visiting a Gurdwara

Sikhs will be pleased if you want to visit a gurdwara. Though some Christians from a Sikh background do not like to do so. Be sensitive about asking them to take you. Learn as much as you can about Sikhism before going. Then contact the secretary and ask for permission to visit, especially if a group want to go together. Remember the gurdwara is a special place for Sikhs and behave respectfully. Dress modestly. Trousers are most acceptable for women. When you reach the entrance take off your shoes and cover your head with a scarf or handkerchief. This applies to both men and women. Make sure you have no tobacco or alcohol with you. If possible do not even have the smell of them on your breath. If you visit when worship is not in progress you will probably find a number of older men sitting round on the floor talking. Greet them politely, placing your hands together at chest level and bowing slightly. If possible, say 'Sat sri akal' as you do so. You may walk up to the platform on which the Granth Sahib rests, but do not bow to it as Sikhs do.

If you go at a time of worship men and boys should sit on the floor with the other men, and women and girls with the women. This applies to married couples as well as single people. If you have small children with you they should sit with their mothers. Women should be careful to sit modestly, preferably with legs crossed. People will come and go during the service so you can feel free to leave when you wish. However it is good to stay to the conclusion of the service if you can. At this time you will be offered some kara prasad. Whether you accept it or not is a matter for your own conscience. It is not food offered to idols. The most questionable matter is whether one bows on receiving it as Sikhs do. Afterwards you will be invited to join in the meal in the langar. Do so if you can. Sikhs will see it as mark of respect and friendship. Wash your hands before eating as you will not usually receive cutlery. Watch how your fellow worshippers eat with their fingers and do the same. Do not despise them for this. It is not a more primitive way of behaving, just a different custom. You will be given the opportunity to wash your hands afterwards.

Ask permission if you want to take photographs or make tape recordings. After your visit a thank you letter will be appreciated.

Useful video tapes showing Sikh life and worship are available from many of the sources listed at the back of the book. Seeing one of these before your visit will help you to understand what is happening.

Things to do

1. Visit a Sikh gurdwara if you can using the guide-lines given in this chapter

2. Ask a Sikh who grew up in India if his devotional life has changed in any way since coming to Britain. Ask if these are significant or just a different way of doing things.

3. Obtain a video of the life of Jesus and invite Sikh friends to come and watch it with you. A Punjabi video is available from the Jesus Film Project in the U.S.A. See the address list at the back of the book. Serve some light vegetarian refreshments at the end and use the opportunity to ask them what they thought of the film.

4. After visiting a gurdwara with Sikh friends, invite them to visit the church in which you worship. This may lead to a discussion of how God dwells in a human heart rather than the place in which people worship.

Chapter 8

WORSHIP AND PRAYER

Private Worship

A Sikh should be consistent in studying scripture and meditating on God. He should also develop a love for the Gurus' teaching and be active in serving the community.

A devout Sikh rises early in the morning and has a bath in running water. Then he wraps himself round in a blanket, shawl or sheet, and closes his eyes to help him shut his mind to visible distractions. He next repeats the word 'Waheguru' (Wonderful Lord) for as long as he can. He may use a woollen cord, with 108 knots for this. As he says 'Waheguru' he passes a knot through his fingers. Sikhs say it is more than a repetition of words. It is a way of knowing the God who already resides within the person. This is the practice known as nam simran (p. 71). Its aim is to call God to mind so deeply that the worshipper's whole life is permeated with him.

After that he recites the Japji and perhaps the Jap of Guru Gobind Singh, and a few other scriptures. Many Sikhs know the Japji by heart and recite it as they are getting ready for work or while doing household chores. Some read it from a prayer book called a gutka. Many families these days listen to it on tape.

Many Sikhs visit the gurdwara in the morning. There they bow before the Granth Sahib and make an offering, before continuing on their way to work.

If a Sikh is free during the day he may visit the gurdwara or read more scripture and pray at home. He will also pray at sunset and when he goes to bed. This daily prayer programme is known as nitnam. Many Sikhs do not perform it fully but do as much as time and opportunity permit.

Sikh prayer may be said standing, kneeling or sitting, facing any direction and at any time of day. A person need not stop work to pray. Even if the work requires mental concentration Sikhs believe the presence of God can be felt in the subconscious.

Corporate worship and prayer

Every Sikh should take part in this. Ideally it should take place every day. There is no weekly holy day. In India where many Sikhs are farmers the moon and the seasons are more important than particular days of the week. Sikhs often gather for worship on the day of the new moon.

Sikh worship has no strict liturgical pattern. It may last 15 minutes or two hours. There are no ordained ministers. Any man or woman who can read the Guru Granth Sahib may conduct a service. To avoid disorder the gurdwara committee usually organises it. Sometimes a granthi is appointed to supervise the gurdwara. He may be concerned with the religious activities or be more like a caretaker. He does not have pastoral responsibilities as a priest does.

In Britain most Sikhs gather for worship on Sundays when they are free from work. The service starts about 9 a.m. though not many people arrive so early. They stand when the Guru Granth Sahib is brought in. It is always carried in on someone's head before being placed on a stand in front of the congregation.

The singing of kirtan takes up most of the service. This consists of hymns sung to a musical accompaniment. A tabla, a type of drum, and a small harmonium are most commonly used. Sometimes violins, and other Indian stringed and percussion instruments are also played. However the emphasis is not on the instruments but the words and the teaching they contain. Before the singing of the hymns one of the musicians may read it and explain its meaning. Sometimes three or four groups of musicians take part in turn. The congregation sometimes joins in the singing but many prefer just to listen and meditate. Some Sikhs say that if you listen attentively to the singing you can experience real peace of mind. Well-known groups of musicians sometimes come from India, East Africa or other parts of Britain. Some members of the congregation record their words and music and meditate on them again during the week.

The singing of kirtan is usually interspersed with talks. Religious or historical poetry may be read. People who take part in these activities feel they are serving God and fellow Sikhs. A giani (a scholar of Punjabi language and literature) will often give a sermon lasting 15 or 20 minutes. He is highly respected in the Sikh community because he can explain the meaning of the Sikh scriptures. All of them consist of poetry and many Sikhs find them hard to understand without help.

The conclusion of the service is the same throughout the world. The first six verses from the Anand (Guru Amar Das's Hymn of Bliss) are recited. The congregation sits for this. Then one person sitting behind the Guru Granth Sahib reads the epilogue of the Japji. The worshippers then stand, place their hands together, bow their heads slightly and intone one verse of the Sukhmani of Guru Arjan.

After that the great congregational prayer, the Ardas, is recited by a member of the congregation. He or she stands in the front facing the Guru Granth Sahib. The congregation joins in at the end of each section by saying, ' Waheguru'.

The Ardas ('a petition to a superior') begins and/or ends every ritual. It takes about 15 minutes to recite and has three parts.

Part one calls to mind the achievements of the ten Gurus and other people important in Sikh history and invokes their blessing.

Part two asks God's forgiveness for the sins of both the individual and the community. Then it pleads for the grace of God and his enlightenment so that members of the congregation may lead a virtuous life. This section ends with a plea for God's blessing on all humanity.

Part three gives time for the special needs of the congregation to be presented to God. These may include prayer for a couple married during the service, a family recently bereaved, people going on journeys to other countries or anything else important to members of the congregation.

At the end of these prayers the congregation bows and the granthi speaks a passage of scripture summing up Sikh beliefs. Then he recites a couplet from scripture, opens the Guru Granth Sahib at random and recites a short passage found there. This is known as vak lao, taking advice from the Guru through his word.

Then kara prasad is served. This is a cooked mixture of semolina, sugar, water and ghee (clarified butter). During the Ardas it will have been marked with a sword as a way of blessing it. The congregation sits while it is distributed. They receive it with their hands cupped together, the right hand being on top. They eat it straight away (p. 79). The word prasad or parshad means a gift. It symbolises the teaching that no one must leave the gurdwara hungry. It may be taken home to share with those too infirm or elderly to come to the gurdwara. Eating together is also a way of showing that the worshippers are one united family of equals. Prasad is not a sacrament. Sikhs do not believe in sacraments.

Weekday worship in the gurdwara

Before dawn each day the Japji is recited and the Guru Granth Sahib brought down from the room where it is kept at night. It is opened at random for vak lao, a reading of the first complete verse on the left hand page. This is the thought for the day. It is displayed on a notice board, usually in the hall of the gurdwara, where everyone can read it.

Anybody who can read Gurmukhi may come into the gurdwara during the day and read the Granth Sahib. Some people come to say their own private prayers.

At sunset the evening prayer, the Sodar Rahiras, is read to mark the end the day.

Sometimes on a weekday evening visiting musicians sing religious songs. Many members of the congregation come to hear them.

The last prayer recited at night is the Kirtan Sohilla. Afterwards the Guru Granth Sahib is put to rest. At the end of each of these prayers Ardas is always offered and kara prasad served to anyone who is present at the time.

Manual work

Sikhs believe that manual work is the highest form of worship. No work is unworthy, though some activities are forbidden. These include running a betting club, dating prostitutes, growing or selling tobacco, trading in alcoholic drinks and begging. However a number of Sikh men have begun to drink since coming to live in Britain, so you may see them in pubs.

Things to do

1. Ask a Sikh friend of the same sex if you can pray together for any particular needs he or she has.

2. Get some copies of John's gospel in English and Gurmukhi to give to Sikh friends. The Bible Society can supply these. South Asian Concern has a literature department with other useful books in Asian languages. Both their addresses can be found at the back of the book.

3. If your friends read English give them copies of a biography of *Sadhu Sundar Singh* or other Christians from a Sikh background.

Chapter 9

CEREMONIES

Name giving

Sikhism states that every child born, boy or girl, is to be welcomed as a gift from God. As soon as possible after a baby's birth the mother will come to the gurdwara to give thanks. There a bowl of amrit, sugar crystals dissolved in water, will be prepared. Then the granthi recites the first five verses of the Japji and strikes the amrit with a two-edged sword, called a khanda. He puts a little amrit on the baby's tongue with the tip of the khanda, and sprinkles some on its face and head. The mother drinks the rest. The Guru Granth Sahib is then opened at random. The initial letter of the first word on the left hand page is that with which the baby's name should begin. To this is added the name Singh, meaning 'lion' for a boy or Kaur, meaning 'princess', for a girl. When the name has been decided the granthi announces it to the congregation who reply 'Sat Sri Akal' (God is eternal). Some scriptures are then read, prayer offered and kara prasad shared. The family usually brings a gift of a piece of brocade about a metre long as a rumala for the Guru Granth Sahib. They also offer money for the making of kara prasad. Sometimes a family requests a reading of the complete Guru Granth Sahib in their home.

Social customs associated with a birth

In most homes the mother will eat a special sweet preparation to help her recover her strength. Though the official Sikh teaching is that babies are to be welcomed regardless of sex, families are generally very pleased if it is a boy but not so happy if it is a girl. Having a girl is expensive as she will need a dowry when she gets married. In India there is no state pension and boys are expected to care for their parents when they are elderly. Girls cannot do this as they belong to their husband's family once they are married. Though elderly people do receive a pension in Britain the family traditions about their care continue in many cases. After the birth, someone in the family will go out and buy Indian sweets, known as ladoos, to give to visitors. But if the baby is a girl they may not bother. Friends and relatives will come to visit, bearing gifts. Sometimes, though, they may not give even simple good wishes for a girl. In joint families the baby is usually born in the husband's family home. The wife's parents visit her and give gifts, usually clothes, to her and her mother-in-law, as well as turban lengths to her father-in-law and brothers-in-law. They may take the mother and baby to their home for up to six weeks.

Uncles, aunts and more distant relatives bring clothes for the baby and in return are usually entertained with tea and Indian sweets. The child's father also gives gifts such as saris, salwar kameez, turban lengths and shirts to various relatives. Custom dictates which and how much particular family members receive.

Five respected men in the Sikh community may be invited to pray for the child. They will receive a meal, a turban length and money. Occasionally the father will wash their hands as they leave. As a sign that children are a gift from God, the father also gives money to charity.

Birthday parties are not part of Indian custom but in Britain many families have taken over the British custom of celebrating in this way.

The proper prefix by which to address an adult is Sirdar (Mr.) or Sardarni (Mrs.) If you are speaking to a man or woman whose name you don't know use bhai-ji or bahin-ji instead.

Initiation

Although anyone born of Sikh parents is a Sikh he is not a full member of the Sikh brotherhood known as the Khalsa until initiated. This can happen any time after he is 14. The ceremony is known as Amrit Pahul and was introduced by Guru Gobind Singh on Baisakhi Day 1699 (p. 44). It is still popular to have initiation on that day.

A candidate should possess the five K'S (p. 93f), accept the doctrines of Sikhism and be attempting to follow the Sikh way of life.

Amrit Pahul is performed by 5 Khalsa members, called the panj pyare. This name goes back to the first 5 Sikhs who were initiated by Guru Gobind Singh (p. 45). No one is present but them, the granthi and the candidates. The granthi opens the Guru Granth Sahib.

One of the five panj pyare explains the principles of the Sikh faith and asks the candidates if they accept them. They make a vow to follow the teachings of the Gurus and Ardas (p. 86) is then offered. A prayer for the preparation of the amrit follows. The granthi then reads a passage of scripture. The panj pyare kneel around the iron bowl containing the amrit. One by one they stir it with a khanda (sword) as they recite the Japji, the Jap of Guru Gobind Singh and the last part of the Anand. The recitation takes about two hours. Then the panj pyare lift up the bowl while one of them offers another prayer.

After that the candidates come forward, one by one, and kneel before the bowl. Each is asked to say, 'The Khalsa is of God, the victory is to God'. Then they are given a handful of amrit to drink. Amrit is also sprinkled on their eyes and hair. If any is left after all the candidates have been initiated they drink it from the bowl. Then the panj pyare repeat the Mool Mantra five times. The senior one talks to the initiates about keeping the teaching of the Gurus, praying daily and following the rules of conduct. These include not cutting the hair on any part of their body, abstaining from alcohol, drugs, adultery and not marrying their sons or daughters for financial gain. The ceremony ends with a reading of the Anand and an offering of Ardas followed by vak lao and kara prasad, which all the initiates eat from the same dish.

THE 5 K'S

These are the insignia of the Khalsa brotherhood which the initiates wear for the rest of their lives, and are worn by all its members, men and women:-

kes or Kesh	is the uncut hair on a person's head and face. Men cover it with a turban, women with a dupatta or chunni.
Kara	is the steel bangle worn on the right wrist. It reminds the wearer of his unity with God and the Khalsa brotherhood.
Kacha	are the pair of shorts now worn as underwear. They were introduced, instead of the loose, longer garments previously worn by men, to allow the wearer freedom in battle.
Kirpan	is the steel sword and is about ten inches long. Sikhs started to wear it when under threat from the Moghuls. It reminded them of their duty to defend the weak and uphold the truth. It was worn in the belt but a miniature version is now more usually worn as a charm round a person's neck.
Kangha	is the small comb made of wood or ivory, though nowadays sometimes of plastic. It enables the Sikh to care for his hair and keep it healthy.

Amrit Pahul has been called Sikh baptism but this is an inadequate description. Baptism is a sacrament and Sikhs do not believe in sacraments. Unlike baptism

Amrit Pahul can be repeated. If a Khalsa Sikh breaks one of his vows and is prepared to confess it to the sangat he can be forgiven. He may be required to do some service to demonstrate his repentance. He may serve in the langar, keep the gurdwara and its surroundings tidy and so on. After a serious lapse, such as unbelief or rejecting Sikh doctrines and practices, he may make a fresh start by undergoing another Amrit Pahul.

Marriage

Sikhs believe that God ordained marriage for every person, so few Sikhs remain single. Sikh parents feel that their son or daughter should marry a Sikh so that they will carry on the Sikh traditions. Normally an older daughter should be married before her sisters. A young person doing higher education may wait until after graduation. If his father has died an older brother should wait till his younger brothers and sisters have finished their education and the girls been married.

Most Sikh parents, even in Britain, want to arrange their son or daughter's marriage. For this reason unmarried young people rarely mix with the opposite sex or, if they do, don't let the older members of their family know. When the parents feel the time has come for a young person to be married they will look for a partner whose character, temperament, age, social status, financial position, appearance and accomplishments make him or her a good match for their child. In traditional families the bride goes to live with her husband and his family so her parents will be anxious for her to be received kindly and to encounter a similar way of life to that in her own home. A couple should not be related within five generations on either their mother's or father's side nor have the same surname. However the prospective partner is often known to some members of the family and belongs to the same caste. Sikhs still observe some caste restrictions, especially where marriage is concerned, despite the Gurus teaching against it. Even the younger generation may do so.

The entire extended family are usually involved in the organisation and expense of a marriage. They may use a middle man who will search for a suitable partner. When he tells them he has found someone both sets of parents meet. The bride's parents may invite the boy and his family for a cup of tea before making a decision. These days the two young people concerned are usually allowed to meet and talk for a while. Though they may do so in a different room from the parents, another brother or sister is usually present. Couples rarely have a completely private meeting. They will probably already have met on a number of occasions in company and be fully informed about the other's interests and life style. After the parents have met they will usually ask the boy or girl for their opinion. If they raise objections the procedure will be terminated and the search starts again.

Sikhs in the West find it difficult to fulfil all the traditional obligations involved in arranging a marriage. The places in which they have settled are widely scattered so that it is difficult to pursue lines of enquiry. Parents often look to relations and friends in the Punjab for help.

An engagement sometimes precedes a marriage but is not essential and not religious. The parents on both sides prepare expensive clothes and gold jewellery for the bride.

The Wedding ceremony

It can happen anywhere where the Guru Granth Sahib is present but usually takes place in a gurdwara. First the groom's family are formally received by the bride's, though the bride herself will not be present. She will be waiting in a different room. A few senior male members of the respective families greet each other and exchange gifts, father with father, elder brother with elder brother etc. The gifts are usually turban lengths and they emphasise the joining, not just of the couple concerned, but of the entire families. The ceremony is called milni and is followed by tea and finger food.

The wedding ceremony proper begins with the morning hymn after which the groom stands before the Guru Granth Sahib. He wears a gold or pink turban. The bride comes in and stands at his left. She is attended by friends or an older sister. She wears a red or pink salwar kameez, embroidered in red or pink and gold, and gold jewellery. Her chunni may almost cover her face. The person conducting the ceremony asks the couple and their parents to stand while he gives them good advice about their marriage and asks God to bless it. Then the bride and groom give public assent to their union by bowing to the Granth Sahib. The bride's father garlands the groom and ties the chunni at the end of the bride's headdress to the scarf which hangs from the groom's shoulder. The gesture indicates that he is handing over responsibilty for his daughter to the bridegroom and his family. The scarf, which is usually pink, may be be sewn up at the end and contain a coconut. The granthi and the musicians then begin to sing the Lavan or wedding hymn. As each of the four verses is sung the couple circle the Granth Sahib clockwise with the groom leading. They come back to their places as each verse comes to an end and bow to the Granth Sahib in confirmation of their vow. On the fourth verse the wedding guests may throw confetti over them. After the Anand and Ardas have been said they seek the Guru's counsel with vak lao and kara prasad is served.

Because the language of the ceremony is not in modern Punjabi, most young people born in Britain do not understand the vows they are making. Some times for their sake and that of non-Sikh guests some-one translates it into English.

Afterwards the guests are entertained in the bride's home, the gurdwara's dining room or a local hall hired for the occasion. Before the meal there may be an entertainment. The bhangra will probably be danced to lively Punjabi music. In the Punjab it is usually the women who dance but in Britain one may see boys and girls dancing together. After the meal the groom's family take the bride away to live in their home. This leave taking of the bride's family is known as the doli.

Death

Sikhs believe that death is God's will. Unlike Hindus who believe that eternal life means being absorbed into God, they prefer to think of it as life in God's presence.

When friends and relations hear of a person's death they try to reach the family home as soon as possible. They also go to the gurdwara to pray for the deceased. On the day of the death no cooking is done in the house of the bereaved. Friends and relatives bring in the food and look after the children.

Before the cremation the family wash and dress the body. They make sure he is wearing the five K's. All the family and friends attend the funeral. Sikhs recognise the place of feelings and the need to express grief when someone dies, but they discourage the wailing which often happens at Hindu funerals. Ardas is said before the procession accompanying the body leaves the house for the gurdwara. There the Granth Sahib is already being read through. After an hour or so the mourners go on to the crematorium. Some families do not go to the gurdwara first but straight to the crematorium where the granthi recites the Kirtan Sohilla, the last prayer of the day. The congregation join him in repeating the Ardas. Special prayers for the soul's everlasting peace are offered and then the body is cremated. Everyone then goes to the gurdwara where the granthi reads the special passage about death from the Granth Sahib and finishes with the Anand, Ardas and vak lao. Kara prasad is then served.

When Sikhs first arrived in Britain they tried scattering the ashes in local rivers but people objected. So now some throw them in a field, some bury them, some send them to Amritsar to be thrown in a river there, some do nothing.

Friends and relatives continue to visit the mourners for a few days after the funeral. A white sheet is spread on the carpet in the room where the bereaved receive them. Everyone takes off their shoes at the door and sits on the sheet. The complete Guru Granth Sahib will probably be read through over a period of about ten days. Members of the family who can read take part in this and everyone sits and listens. They believe they gain strength from God during this time and learn to accept his will. This complete reading is known as Sahaj Path. When it is finished the bereaved and their friends gather, usually at the gurdwara. There they sing hymns about death and pray that the departed soul may have peace. Sikhs wear white, not black, when mourning. They do so until the ashes have been taken to their resting place. Until then they consider the person's spirit to be in a state of unrest. After that the dead person should not be remembered any more because the soul will have been reborn. Sikhs emphasise that men and women should concentrate, not on mourning the dead, but on loving the living.

Things to do

1. If Sikh friends invite you to attend one of their ceremonies, attend if possible. Stay the full time if you can. You will learn a great deal that way.

2. If Sikh neighbours are preparing for the marriage of a son or daughter, find a suitable time to ask them about the meaning of the marriage ceremony.

3. Ask Sikh friends about their ways of mourning and expressing grief. Be prepared to share the Christian attitude if appropriate.

Chapter 10

FESTIVALS

The Sikh calendar is based on the phases of the moon, so the dates of festivals vary from year to year. The gurdwaras publish an almanac giving the dates for the year in question. In India they often happen on a weekday but in Britain this is inconvenient so the festival is usually held on the nearest Sunday to the actual day.

A feature of most festivals is the continuous reading of the Guru Granth Sahib, known as akhand path. It takes about 48 hours, starting two days before the festival and being completed before dawn on the actual day. Readers work in spells of no more than two hours each. Members of the Sikh community come to listen when they can.

Akhand path is performed on all important occasions in the family and community. In the home Sahaj Path, the broken reading, is more common. Both are reminders that Sikhs are deeply attached to their scriptures which are their guide and comfort in every aspect of their lives.

As many people as possible come to the gurdwara early on the morning of the festival day and listen to the reading of the last five pages of the Guru Granth

Sahib. Then follow readings, prayers, and hymns about the life of the Guru whose festival is being celebrated. At the end of the service kara prasad is served.

In India, and sometimes in Britain, the Guru Granth Sahib is carried through the streets on a decorated lorry. The worshippers follow, led by the five panj pyare. Bands play joyful music. There are usually competitions and sports with prizes. Prominent speakers may come from a long distance.

In Britain most festivals are held inside the gurdwara because of the climate!

Baisakhi

This assembly of Sikhs to worship God and listen to the teachings of the Guru was introduced by Guru Amar Das in the 16th century. It usually happens on April 13th, the beginning of the Sikh New Year. After 1699 Baisakhi assumed a new importance because, at the festival in that year, Guru Gobind Singh initiated the Khalsa and baptised its first five members (p. 44). Each year on this day the old flag on the gurdwara is replaced by a new one.

In 1919 the British Government introduced restrictive measures throughout India, to curb the disturbances happening in some places. All meetings were banned. At Baisakhi a large number of country people began to gather in Amritsar. In the heat of midday, many of them went to rest in the Jallianwala Bagh, an open space in the centre of the city. Some political leaders took the opportunity to speak to these people but General Dyer, who was in charge of the army in

Amritsar, saw it as a violation of the law against public meetings. He marched his soldiers into the Jallianwala Bagh and, without warning, ordered them to fire into the crowd. There was only one exit to the garden, that through which the soldiers had come. Panic ensued. 379 people were killed and over 2,000 injured. This incident did irreparable damage to Sikh-British relationships and a new nationalist organisation, the Central Sikh League was formed to oppose British rule. The story of the Jallianwala Bagh has been passed down the generations. It is vividly portrayed in Richard Attenborough's film, 'Gandhi'. Many Sikhs feel deeply about the massacre. Be sensitive to the feelings of any of them who tell you about it.

Diwali

This festival is popular in Britain but in India celebration is usually confined to the Golden Temple in Amritsar. It takes place at the end of October or the beginning of November, depending on the phases of the moon. Diwali celebrates light and deliverance. In Amritsar the Golden Temple is illuminated, a firework display is held and the temple treasures are on show for about two hours.

In India the gurdwara is lit with wick lamps but in Britain Sikhs illuminate their houses as well as the gurdwara, using small electric lights or candles. They place them outside, on window sills, above the door and on garden fences. In places where many Sikhs live the streets are lined with hundreds of lights.

Diwali is celebrated by Hindus too but the stories associated with it are quite different.

Sikhs remember an incident in the life of Guru Hargobind, the 6th Guru. An officer of the Moghul emperor, Jehangir, had imprisoned him in the fort at Gwalior. His official crime was the non-payment of a fine imposed on his father. But the officer also suspected him of treason because he had raised his own army. Guru Hargobind appealed to the Emperor who examined his case personally. He ordered the release of Hargobind. But 52 Hindu princes were sharing the Guru's imprisonment and he declared that he would only accept his freedom if they were also released. Jehangir replied that as many princes as could pass through a narrow passage holding on to Hargobind's clothes would be released. The Guru ordered a cloak with long tassel-like ends to be brought. Every one of the princes walked to freedom holding on to the train.

Gurpurbs

These festivals remind Sikhs of important events in the lives of the Gurus. The birthday of Guru Nanak is celebrated in November and that of Guru Gobind Singh in December. The martyrdom of the fifth Guru, Arjan, is remembered in May or June. Some gurdwaras offer fruit to passers-by on that day. Sikhs also remember the martyrdom of Guru Tegh Bahadur, the ninth Guru, and the sons of Guru Gobind Singh.

Things to do

1. Ask a Sikh friend to tell you how he celebrates Baisakhi or Diwali.

2. Invite a Sikh friend to come with you to church for Christmas or Easter. Arrange a meeting place on the way or call for him. A few days beforehand tell him the story of what we are celebrating and explain what will happen at the service. This will help him to feel less strange.

3. Consider arranging an alternative 'Christian' Diwali for Asian Christians and others. 'Light' and 'Deliverance' are also great Christian themes. Such a Diwali could be used in evangelism too.

Chapter 11

DAILY LIFE OF MOST SIKHS

In India and Pakistan the turban is a common form of headgear for men, whatever their religion. But in Britain it has become associated particularly with Sikhism. The Gurus encouraged men to wear it partly to prevent non-Sikhs being picked on and treated as Sikhs in times of persecution and partly to prevent their less courageous followers from deserting. Sikhs should wear a turban even if they are bald headed.

It is formed from a piece of cloth about 5.5 metres long and 45 centi-metres wide and may be of any colour. For young boys a turban is shorter. Turbans are starched so they will keep their shape. A well tied turban can be worn several times before it loses its shape and needs washing. Under the turban the hair is tied into a topknot called a jura. It is sometimes covered with a small square of cloth, like a handkerchief, called a rumal. The beard is tied up in a special way, using a kind of glue and a piece of material like very fine net. Most Sikh men are very proud to wear a turban even though it is not one of the five Ks. One Sikh from East Africa said, 'There's no way I would give up my turban, that's for sure. I'd rather die or get out, but I'd maintain my turban and my faith'.[1]

A small boy's hair is plaited and kept in place by ribbons. When he is a little older he graduates to a topknot and later to a turban. Boys start wearing turbans at the age of about seven. A boy's first turban is tied by a granthi in the presence of the Granth Sahib, with his family and friends watching.

The rest of a male Sikh's clothing is usually western though some older men may wear Indian clothes; usually a pair of churidar pyjamas (tight fitting trousers) and a kurta (a loose shirt). Some also wear the achkan, a knee length tailored jacket.

Sikh women wear the salwar kameez, a loose top and trousers, tight or baggy as the fashion of the moment happens to be. They throw a scarf, known as a chunni, round their shoulders. The chunni traditionally represents a woman's honour. In the presence of male relatives of her husband and in the gurdwara a woman pulls it over her head. Sikh women wear the kacchi, the shorts, as well as men.

Purdah, the custom of women being veiled in public, was denounced by the Gurus. It is not practised in Britain but, in some villages in the Punjab, a woman must pull her chunni right over her face so that it becomes a sort of veil.

All Sikhs should adopt the role of householder when they reach adult years so marriage is expected of every individual. The strength of a marriage is believed to be basic to the partners' growth in faith. Both should work for a complete identity of interests.

Any sexual relationship outside marriage is considered abhorrent. A marriage is more than the physical coming together of a man and a woman. It is a spiritual union too.

Divorce is discouraged but possible. Widows may remarry but if they don't they are respected and allowed to play a full part in the life of the family and community. A widow may also be the head of a family with her eldest son carrying out her decisions. When her husband dies a single younger brother-in-law may sometimes marry the widow.

Traditionally the mother is the queen of the house and the father the breadwinner. Older women do not use their husband's name when talking about him. They often use the term sardar-ji – 'ji' is commonly used as a form of respect. A young man may say uncle-ji, sister-ji etc when addressing an older member of the family. In India most women retain their maiden name after marriage, though sometimes mothers-in-law give them a new first name. Abroad they usually add their husband's surname to avoid confusion.

In theory men and women are regarded as equal; in practice it is not fully so. Women may conduct ceremonies, sing hymns or speak in the gurdwara but do not always eat with men in the langar. Men take a full part in preparing and serving the food though. Most Sikh congregations are dominated by men though women do serve on management committees sometimes. In some gurdwaras they have even become presidents or secretaries. Though women are permitted to read the Guru Granth Sahib only a minority actually do so. Most gurdwaras have an istri sabha, a women's association, where the women arrange their own activities. In the Midlands there is a gurdwara entirely run by women. But, on the whole, women play a subordinate role in the Sikh community. If you ask a Sikh man why, he will probably tell you that women are too busy with household chores to have time for other activities.

In India sons usually bring their wives to live in the family home but abroad each sub-group of parents and children often have an independent home. However the senior members of the extended family are still consulted over important matters. Their views are respected and when discussion is over the final decision is left to them.

Sikhs do not appreciate physical demonstrations of love in public, even between husband and wife. Sexual matters are not discussed openly. However older sisters and aunts discuss the facts of life freely with the teenage girls of a family. Courtship is out of the question and girls are expected to maintain the honour of the family by remaining virgins until they are married. But men are forgiven if they sow a few wild oats. Most Sikhs do not object to the use of contraceptives by married people but the older members of a family become anxious if a young couple do not have a child within a year or two of marriage.

Though Sikhism rejects caste it has never succeeded in completely shaking it off. Guru Amar Das introduced the langar in an attempt to remove caste distinctions. However, in the Punjab, members of different caste groups live in separate villages, marry each other and mix rarely. Abroad they eat together in the langar, worship and eat kara prasad together but still usually arrange marriages between members of the same sub-group.

In Britain, Sikhs of different groups find themselves living in the same street and working in the same factory. They usually, though not always, mix together happily. Some groups do not shave and keep their turbans and the 5 Ks. Others consider shaving acceptable. Some adopt a halfway position, wearing the long hair, beard and bracelet but compromising in other respects. Many drink alcohol, though orthodox Sikhism forbids it. Others are strictly against smoking, also forbidden to a good Sikh. They may be vegetarian too. Tensions do sometimes arise between Sikhs holding these divergent views. It is hard for someone from a family where uncut hair and a turban are the rule to mix with a person who covers their short hair with a handkerchief in the gurdwara and smells of tobacco. Sometimes separate gurdwaras are established to accommodate people with these different practices.

The official Sikh position regarding vegetarianism is far from clear. Some Sikhs never eat meat, eggs or fish. For most only beef is taboo. In the langars meat is never served to avoid embarrassing anyone. The Gurus did not state that Sikhs should be vegetarians. But many Indians believe that meat causes such things as bad temper, high blood pressure and cancer and are vegetarians for these kinds of reasons. Guru Nanak said that it is not being vegetarian or non-vegetarian that matters but moral purity. A God-centred life is the only guarantee of that.

A Sikh who uses alcohol, drugs, except as medicine, and tobacco is not allowed to sit on a gurdwara committee. In some gurdwaras they are excluded from the sangat till they mend their ways. When they do they may be required to do penance. This will usually be a form of public service, such as cleaning the shoes of the congregation. Both the Gurdwara Act of 1925 and the Delhi Gurdwara Act of 1971 state that a Sikh who uses tobacco cannot be on the electoral role of his gurdwara. In Britain Sikhs do not generally give or receive wine or spirits as presents. Occasionally they will give them to Anglo-Saxon friends, thinking they appreciate them.

The Gurus declared that fasting, abstaining from certain foods or eating certain others is not a way to blessing. They denounced extreme asceticism and fasting over a long period of time, maintaining that a healthy human body is necessary for work, prayer and service.

In the early days of Sikhism the Gurus were anxious that their followers should not slip back into Hinduism so they did lay down various prohibitions: no Sikh should take part in any form of idolatry; they should have nothing to do with ideas of pollution and ritual purity, black magic, horoscopes and other superstitious practices; they should not wear the Hindu sacred thread, take bribes, paint signs on their foreheads, pray at the grave of holy men, go on pilgrimages or visit places holy to other religions. The books of other religions may be read with profit but faith must be based on the Sikh scriptures. Sikhs should not gamble, steal or commit adultery.

Work

Every able-bodied person has a moral duty to do some useful work for society. A Sikh may not beg or excuse himself from working on the pretext that he is devoting his time to worship and meditation. It does not matter what form of work a person does but it must not involve deceit. Doing manual or menial work is nothing to be ashamed of. Immoral or illegal dealing is disgraceful, so a Sikh should not approve of or produce alcohol or drugs nor promote pornography or prostitution.

The Gurus commended the creation of wealth by legitimate means but denounced the love of money for its own sake, or gaining it by depriving others. Sikhs must live only on money earned honestly and be generous to charity. This does not mean just giving away their surplus but foregoing or cutting down on their own needs. God gave gifts to all men but they should not use them just for their own pleasure. They should give them away for common use. This calls for sacrifice. Guru Amar Das stated that Sikhs should give one tenth of their money as service to the community. There is no system for collecting gifts. What a Sikh gives is a matter for his or her own conscience.

Things to do

1. When a Sikh family has a new baby visit them taking a small gift. Clothes are very acceptable.

2. Get together with a group of Asian Christians for an evening of Bhangra dancing. You could do this for Diwali. Be careful to find out the meaning of the songs beforehand as some can be sexist, rude or provocative.

3. Invite a Sikh family to join you for a day out at the seaside or in the country. If you plan a picnic ask them beforehand if there are any foods they don't eat. In particular, *don't prepare anything containing beef*. And don't take along any alcoholic drinks. This will avoid embarassment. Take something with which to clean the hands before and after eating.

Chapter 12

SIKHS IN BRITAIN

The Sikh community in Britain has proved itself adaptable. Most families were landowners in the Punjab but here they have become labourers, skilled workers and businessmen. Others study to become doctors, dentists and lawyers. Most Sikhs prefer to work for themselves rather than be employed by someone else. As soon as they have amassed enough capital many buy businesses; garages, warehouses, factories and shops. Some have become insurance agents, driving instructors, social workers, teachers, policemen. The list is endless.

Family and Community Loyalty

Sikhs have kept their distinctiveness as an ethnic group to a large extent and maintained a strong sense of identity. The emphasis on community and family values has been a major factor in this. A family will visit relatives and friends for the weekend at least once a month and may drive long distances to do so. One or two other weekends in the month they will be the hosts, so they have little time to themselves.

The doctrine of sewa has instilled in Sikhs a strong sense of honour and loyalty to one's family, to those from the same village in the Punjab, to friends, to the entire Sikh community. These values are more important than one's personal welfare. If a person sometimes has to be less than honest for the sake of others no one blames him; loyalty is everything. It involves lending money when someone is in need, helping in sickness or bereavement, going out of one's way to make sure others are never left to struggle with burdens alone. Though these may be social obligations they are often based on deep affection. Pride in being a Sikh also plays a part in community loyalty.

Money may be loaned without interest and without a promise to pay it back. Hospitality is offered to others constantly. When a newcomer arrives from India fellow Sikhs will provide him with food and shelter for an indefinite period. They will help him to find a job and expect nothing in return but mutual friendship. When one man's family arrived a friend offered him the use of his cheque book until he found his feet. The friend knew they came from the same area in the Punjab as himself and that community honour would be a kind of collateral.

Even very westernised Sikhs respect their parents and help needy relatives. They often finance the education of younger members of their extended family. They cherish its emotional support and take pride in fulfilling their duty to it.

Family honour (izzat)

This plays a large part in the life of a Sikh. Izzat is the respect society places on individual family groups when they behave in culturally acceptable ways. A family protects its own izzat in every possible way by trying to see that all its members live up to it. The 'bad' behaviour of children can detract from family izzat. The family will be criticised for not enforcing firm discipline. Personal prestige is subordinated to the communal approval of the group. A son may have to forgo the career of his choice if his father feels it would detract from the family's izzat.

Although the Gurus instructed their followers to reject caste, it still plays a part in the life of the Sikh community, especially in marriage. A Sikh from a high caste will usually regard himself as superior to one from a low caste. A high caste family is also more likely to be regarded as 'good' by others in the community. Sikhs of different castes have tended to establish separate gurdwaras in British cities.

In evaluating another member of his community a Sikh will want to find out if they come from a family with a 'good' or 'bad' reputation. The wider community looks to 'good' families for leadership. Even if an individual's behaviour is not up to the expected standard, coming from a 'good' family is to his credit. 'Bad' families can improve their status by serving others.

The importance of having the right contacts

Wealth is a means of maintaining izzat. Wealthy families usually have political and business contacts which can benefit their friends. Such contacts are more valuable than money for they can help people improve their izzat. Marion was frequently asked to put in a word to a prospective Anglo-Saxon employer for an Asian applying for a job, to a headmaster to enrol a boy in his school etc. Often she did not know the authority involved but the applicant who asked thought she must have prestige in the community and that her influence would make a difference. The person making the request usually found it hard to believe that in Britain most jobs are given on merit not influence and that Marion's unwarranted interference might even prejudice the employer against the applicant! Sadly the misunderstanding sometimes meant a cooling of the friendship as Marion's refusal was misread as uncaring.

Because a wealthy family can give more to community projects and charity they are rated more highly than a poorer person who gives all he has. A family's wealth may be displayed in the women's jewellery. A large dowry for daughters may suggest that a family is wealthy and many ordinary families struggle to provide one in order to raise their izzat. On the other hand they may wish to marry a son to a girl brought direct from the Punjab. In this case a plane ticket and £200 may be considered adequate.

In theory all members of the community are responsible for the actions of their fellow members. If someone does not behave properly, he disgraces his family and community. Sikhs believe one person's behaviour reflects on the whole kin group. A Sikh who becomes a Christian faces family and community pressure to recant on a scale which is unknown to most Westerners. One Sikh teenager living in London went to a church youth club where he heard the gospel for the first time. After some months he decided to accept Christ and bought a Bible. When his parents found it in his room and asked about it he admitted that he had become a Christian. They were horrified, took away the Bible and forbad him to go on attending the youth club. He did that but continued to meet Christian friends secretly for Bible study. Inevitably his parents came to know. When they faced him with it he declared that he could not desert Jesus who had given his life for him. At that his parents ordered him to leave home. He did so and went to a Midlands city. There he found a room and work and, eventually, Christian friends, but he still feels the loss of his family keenly. Western Christians should be aware of such consequences when trying to help former Sikhs. They must be prepared to take them into their own family if they are thrown out by their parents.

Older Sikhs are very aware of community opinion and worry about misconduct by the younger generation. Gossip controls a lot of what happens. 'What will people say?' can become the motivation behind all the family's hopes and efforts. Anything that could lower the family's prestige has to be hidden. On the other hand, if a member of the family does something noteworthy his relatives will make a great effort to broadcast it and so improve their image. Older members of a family are particularly concerned about conduct which may prevent their children making a 'good' marriage. The emphasis is not so much on the behaviour itself but on how it will be perceived by the community. Many parents know that their children do not always live up to their standards but are only really concerned if others get to know of their 'misconduct'. If this happens the parents are deeply grieved. They may sometimes become ill; this may be play acting to make a young person feel guilty but sometimes it is genuine.

Most Sikhs value the older members of their family. They feel that their years of experience give them the right to respect and honour. They will consult the elderly whenever the family has a decision to make. Very few Sikhs would put an old person into a home as this would damage the family's izzat.

Conflict between the generations

In spite of group loyalties this does exist. In Britain it is common for young Sikhs to go on to college or university after leaving school, even when their parents are totally uneducated. Parents are usually proud of their children's achievements but worry if they choose a course such as history or art, which they feel will not give them prestige. They prefer a subject which will raise the family's izzat, such as medicine or law. This may result in a clash between the young person and his or her parents. Quite often the sense of loyalty instilled into a Sikh boy or girl from childhood means that they bow to their parents' wishes. Surinder, for instance, wanted to train as a beautician when she left school but her father told her it was out of the question. She must go to a secretarial college. Without any more argument she did as he told her.

Some years ago, when Sally was working in an Asian area of Britain, she and a friend started a club in their home for Asian teenage girls. For a few weeks several came and learnt new craft skills. After a while the numbers dropped and eventually no one came. Later Sally and Barbara learnt that the girls' families did not consider making jewellery or doing tapestry a 'useful' occupation. If they had taught them cooking or sewing, to prepare them for marriage, or coached them in G.C.S.E. subjects, to further a career, they might have been willing to keep on sending them. Pursuing a hobby just for pleasure is not normally part of South Asian culture.

Attitude to girls

A few families still supervise a teenage daughter strictly and confine her to the home unless she goes out with older female relatives. This way they feel she will remain pure and loyal. Others, especially from East Africa, argue for a more western upbringing of girls. They allow them to have the same opportunities as boys for further education and a professional career. Most families adopt a half way position.

Some parents like to see their girls married soon after they leave school. They fear that if they have a taste of independence by going out to work they will no longer be under their control. This may mean that they won't consent to a 'good' marriage i.e. with a partner the parents have chosen. Even when a girl does not want to marry she usually bows to her parents wishes in this respect. On the other hand they are usually happy to delay a boy's marriage until his professional training is complete.

Most boys appreciate what their parents have done for them. They have no intention of forsaking them nor will the parents disown their son. But parents usually think that when a boy wants a love marriage rather than an arranged one he has taken a wrong turning and rejected their judgement. They think of their son's welfare in practical terms; a career with

prestige; financial security rather than personal satisfaction. They often disagree with the development of
self and the pursuit of individual satisfaction learnt in
school, considering it selfish.

Marriage

Primary immigration of Sikhs into Britain has, in
general, stopped. But girls are still brought over from
the Punjab for marriage. A boy's parents often feel
that a girl from the Punjab will encourage their son to
remain loyal to traditional Sikh values. A new
daughter-in-law will be expected to look after her
parents-in-law's every need and to be loyal to them.
Punjabi girls born in Britain usually want more
independence and are not happy to be tied to home
chores. A boy may want to marry an educated girl
who appreciates the western concept of a love
marriage and can provide intellectual company. But
he does want her to be a virgin. At college or
university he sees the way white girls act towards the
opposite sex and assumes that few of them are virgins.
Therefore he feels they are not likely to remain loyal
to a husband.

Courtship is not part of Asian tradition but these
days a few westernised parents do actually allow a
couple to go out together to functions of which they
approve, before any marriage arrangements are made.

Divorce is becoming more common but it is
frowned on and considered a stigma to the family.

Difficulties for young people

Those who have been taught in British schools have
absorbed ideas and practices of western culture. Some

parents who arrived in this country in the 60s and early 70s do not seem to have realised this was inevitable. Now they worry about their children growing away from their inherited traditions. Many young people have only limited Punjabi and so find it difficult to share their ideas, hopes and problems with their parents on any deep level. Young Sikhs like fish and chips, burgers, and pizzas even though they still eat Punjabi food at home. Some girls prefer western to Punjabi dress and like to go out with their contemporaries rather than with the family.

On the other hand some young Sikhs become more ardent in their faith than their elders. They are keen to maintain and live up to their cultural heritage and to prove that the Sikh way of life is superior to all others. Others are in rebellion against what they consider the outmoded standards of behaviour to which the older generation would like them to conform.

Most adopt a lifestyle somewhere between the two. Such young people often live in a cultural vacuum. Their parents may be so busy working that they have no time to see that their children learn Gurmukhi or absorb Sikh values and manners. One young girl pointed to a new but vacant house and said, "See that house? It is beautiful on the outside but there is nothing inside. This is the way it is with us westernised Indians. We wear Indian clothes but there is nothing inside. We feel an emptiness which is only relieved by being active"[1]

One young man said, "Look at Raj. He continually goes to parties and the pub. This is the way in which he escapes from the inner emptiness he feels when he is alone. I feel sorry for him"[2]

Some young people become aggressive. This may be a symptom of deep insecurity.

Not all young people suffer to the same extent. Some families manage to maintain the traditional family culture but their children do often experience some confusion. One girl said, "Why should I go to the gurdwara? I can't understand when they read out of the holy book; and even if I could the women are so busy gossiping that I can't hear anything."[3]

Many older Sikhs have not really faced up to the difficulties of a younger generation brought up in Britain. Nor have the gurdwaras given them much assistance. They hold Gurmukhi classes but only about 25 per cent of young Sikhs attend. Thus worship may be meaningless for them. Arthur Helwig suggests that sooner or later Sikhs in Britain will have to decide if English or Gurmukhi should be the language of worship [4]. So far they have expected everyone to learn Gurmukhi because of the historic relationship between language and culture.

Returning to the Punjab

Older Sikhs have a natural longing for the Punjab. Parents often want to take their children there and may present a glorified picture of village life. Younger people who have never visited do the same thing. But when the youngsters arrive they are disillusioned. One young woman had been married to a man brought over from India for the marriage. He was eager to take her back to his home village for a holiday. Her mother spoke with enthusiasm of how enjoyable such a visit would be. But when the girl arrived she felt stifled by such restrictions as having to cover her face in front of her father-in-law and being expected to refrain from speaking to her husband in company. She hated the lack of privacy too. All the details of what she did were seen and commented on.

Some parents who have brought their families up in Britain pay lipservice to plans of returning to the Punjab to live. But their children, brought up in the materialistic culture of the west, would never be able to adapt. In their heart of hearts the parents know their longing is just a wistful dream.

Personal ownership

In the villages in the Punjab, those who have returned from overseas are thought to be always wealthy and successful. To be a British returnee gives dignity to a person and his family. He may show off by building a large house in his home village even if he never intends to live there.

For a Sikh, owning land gives prestige. He may work in a factory, own a shop etc. but he usually feels unfulfilled if he owns no land. Many Sikh emigrees buy land in the Punjab even though they will never farm it. When a Sikh brings his family to Britain they may have to live in rented accommodation at first but all those of working age will pool their earnings until their dream of buying their own house comes true.

The Sikh Missionary Society

This was founded in Gravesend in 1969, though its headquarters were transferred to Southall, in West London in 1979. It is not an evangelistic organisation as Westerners understand it, but is dedicated to teaching the younger generation of Sikhs to appreciate and adopt the religious and cultural behaviour of their forefathers. It publishes pamphlets and booklets describing Sikh belief and practices. These sometimes use religious language which young people have heard at school or from white British acquaintances. The gurdwara may be referred to as the Sikh church, the Granth Sahib as the Sikh Bible, and Guru Nanak as the Sikh Saviour.

Individualism

These issues are symptoms of what worries older Sikhs deeply: the fact that their young people are absorbing the principle of individualism, prized in western culture but alien to eastern thought. As already pointed out, traditional Asian culture values the welfare of the family and community more highly than that of the individual. This can lead to clashes between children and their families. Though most work through these without outside help, a few young people do appeal to social workers for assistance. This sometimes aggravates the situation. A western social worker will usually uphold the value of individualism and fail to understand the Punjabi concept of group honour. Occasionally a girl may run away from home and in some places hostels have been set up for such people. Most Sikhs strongly disapprove of these. They feel that the welfare services should not assume or undermine parental authority.

Despite all this, rebellion and disobedience are less of a problem among Punjabi than white families. Delinquency and crime are also less common. Most Asian young people work hard at school. Parents encourage their children to do homework and supervise their time and activities carefully.

Some teach their children about the Sikh faith at home. Others look to the gurdwara to do this.

But even young people who are not rebelling against traditional teaching may hesitate about taking amrit because they have not been saying their prayers regularly or wearing the five Ks.

Over 40 per cent of the Sikh community were born in Britain and so are technically British. They may never visit the Punjab yet they say they are Punjabi. Most white British people do not think of them as British. And most British born Sikhs are proud to belong to the Sikh community. It gives them a sense of pride, identity and self-respect. Some men who cut their beards when young so as to be like their white contemporaries are now growing them again. As they have grown older ethnic pride has resurfaced and proved stronger than the desire to identify with white friends.

Maintaining Sikh traditions

Some Sikh men cut their hair on arriving in Britain because they thought it would make it easier to get a job. For many of them it was a deeply emotional issue. One young man tells how when he arrived in Britain his uncle told him he would have to cut his hair. At first he refused. But when his uncle continued to argue with him he gave way. He had his photograph taken beforehand to remind himself of where his real loyalties lay. When the deed had been done he cried all day over the hair which he had saved.

Disputes sometimes occur between liberal and conservative Sikhs. The conservative fight to maintain Sikh symbols, faith and separateness. They may try to introduce restrictions in the gurdwara such as a rule that only unshaved individuals may hold office. But shaved Sikhs do attend the gurdwaras and participate fully in its activities. They often revert to a more traditional role when they marry and try to make their children more conservative than they are themselves.

In the Punjab there is no specific day of the week for Sikh worship but in Britain it normally takes place on Sunday. Nevertheless many elderly Sikhs attend the gurdwara each evening to sing kirtan.

Sikhs usually have open air processions for gurpurbs in India. In Britain they seldom do, partly because of the climate and partly because they feel local white residents may not like it. If the Granth Sahib is to be taken to a home for akhand path it will go by car.

Social life

Gurdwaras have also become the focus of social, as well as religious, activities in a way they never are in the Punjab. Many have libraries with books in both Gurmukhi and English. Sports activities may be organised or coach outings to visit Sikh communities in other cities or places of interest and enjoyment such as Blackpool or Alton Towers.

The turban

As pointed out in the introduction, the characteristic of conservative Sikhs which has attracted most public attention is the turban. They regard wearing one as crucial to their faith. But they have sometimes been ridiculed or victimised for doing so, at least in their own eyes. Struggles with employers, especially in the transport industry, attracted a lot of attention in the early seventies. After considerable pressure, most firms which employ Sikhs have agreed that they may wear their turbans whether there is a requirement for other employees to cover their heads or not. In 1976 Sikhs who ride motor cycles were allowed to wear a turban rather than a crash helmet. Most head teachers now allow Sikh boys to wear a turban at school. On building sites Sikhs still have to wear hard hats though they would like to wear turbans. The other one of the 5 Ks which has been the subject of legislation is the sword or kirpan. Like the Scots' dirk it has been exempted from the rule about carrying offensive weapons.

Alcohol problems

Alcohol abuse has become a problem in certain Sikh families. Some men have found it difficult to cope with living in western society or to work up courage to speak out about the situations in which they find themselves. A number have taken refuge in alcohol. Attempts by outsiders to help such people have run into considerable difficulties because the Sikh community is generally unwilling to acknowledge that the problem exists.

Attitudes of white people

In places with a large Sikh community, some white residents have resented Sikhs who appear to have made a success of establishing themselves in Britain. They have paid cash for their own houses and cars, fly off to visit relatives in different parts of the world, pay for expensive education for their children. White people cannot understand how they have acquired such wealth in a relatively short period of time while they are struggling to make ends meet. They fail to realise that a Sikh family is not toiling alone, as they are, but is part of an extended family which pools its resources. Members who are prospering pay for the needs of those who are not so well off. Most Sikhs are also ambitious. They set their sights high and are willing to live frugally for a time in order to reach their goal.

White residents often view all ethnic minorities as one group with the same problems. Young Sikhs may find themselves classed as 'black' even though their skin is relatively light in colour. They resent this and some feel they have been the subject of racial discrimination. Some white people assume that all second generation immigrants are irresponsible, unemployed, using drugs and sometimes involved in crime. One white woman living in an area where there are many Sikhs said to Marion one day, 'I can't go out at night in case these Indians follow me.' Most Sikh young people are not in the least likely to do so. The authority structure in most Punjabi families is strong. The biggest problem for the Sikh community is how to convince many of their young people that religion is important in a world where materialism is increasingly attractive. They have goals for them – to work hard and do well. And the majority of their children live up to these expectations.

Things to do

1. Find an opportunity to ask a Sikh you know well about any difficulties they are experiencing in bringing up their children in a culture different from their own.

2. Ask how Sikh parents go about arranging the marriage of their children. Then talk about what happens in western culture and discuss the advantages and disadvantages of each. But do not assume that all Sikhs have arranged marriages.

3. If possible talk to a Sikh couple about their wedding. They may be able to show you photographs or a video.

Chapter 13

POINTS OF CONTACT FOR CHRISTIANS

When talking to a Sikh about your Christian faith you will probably find that he agrees with you about many things. Much Sikh teaching is similar to that in Christianity.

A Genuine Search for God

Expressions of devotion and love for God are found throughout the Granth. Often Christians can utter the same words. We can admire the dedication and conviction of countless Sikh martyrs who were prepared to make the supreme sacrifice for their faith. Of course, there are Sikh hypocrites and heretics but the same can be said for Christians.

Concept of God

For Christians and Sikhs the world is no accident. The Bible opens with the statement,

> 'In the beginning God created the heavens
> and the earth'.

The Granth says,

> 'He was in the beginning. He was in the
> primal age. The true one is, was, O Nanak,
> and shall ever be.'

Both religions teach that God is sovereign over history and that the present order will eventually give way to a new one.

They share the belief that God did not set the world in motion and then stand back from it. He is a constantly active God. Nor is He an abstract idea or just a moral force. He is also personal, capable of being loved and honoured and yet everywhere in creation. He may be addressed in such personal terms as Father, Lover, Master. Christians and Sikhs find their reason for living in their relationship with God, whose will they seek to do in their daily lives.

The Word of God

Both religions place great emphasis on Scripture and encourage their followers to read it daily. Christians regard the Bible as the eternal, God-inspired Word. For Sikhs the Granth is not just a 17th century document but the eternal word of God.

For Christians the 'Word' means more than just an utterance. It possesses power. The prophets often speak of the Word, given to them by God, which they must speak out. 'The word of the Lord came to me' (Ezekiel 12:1). The Word is also the instrument of the creator, 'Before the world was created, the Word already existed; he was with God and he was the same as God. From the very beginning the Word was with God. Through him God made all things; not one thing in all creation was made without him.' (John 1:1-3)

The Sikh term for the 'Word' is **Shabad**. It is said to be present in everything, but beyond human discerning. Sikhs believe that the Gurus were inspired by the Word and that their primary function was to tell it to others.

God's plan of Salvation

Both Christians and Sikhs believe that God sent his divinely inspired messengers into the world and that an era of history began with their ministries. Sikhs say that Guru Nanak's birth was divinely ordained. Christians believe that Mary conceived Jesus through the power of the Holy Spirit.

Guru Nanak was conscious of being called and ordained to bring people a revelation of God's truth. He had a sense of mediation, of bridging the gap between God and men by showing them the way to achieve salvation. He taught that it was achieved through meditation.

Jesus was also conscious of being called by God to reveal his truth to mankind. But unlike Guru Nanak he declared that he Himself was the way (John 3:16). He gave his life on the cross to bridge the gap between men and God.

Sikhs believe that the Gurus were inspired by God but deny that God ever assumed human form. 'God has no form or features.' (Ad Granth p. 750)

They are suspicious of any teaching about a God who was born and died as in the stories of the Hindu gods. They are also suspicious of the Christian teaching that Jesus was God incarnate.

The Grace of God

The word grace appears many times in both the Christian and Sikh scriptures. In both it refers to the undeserved gift of God. 'For it is by God's grace that you have been saved through faith. It is not the result of your own efforts, but God's gift... '(Ephesians 2: 8-9). Guru Arjan 'All the works we do to expiate for our sins save us not but the name of the Lord washes off myriads of sins.' Both readings affirm that salvation cannot be gained by good works and insist on the need for a changed life.

But we must treat the word grace carefully. Despite the references in the Granth which appear to mean that man cannot do anything to save himself, Sikhs do not view grace as the exclusive means by which they may obtain salvation. Some view it as merely God's reward in response to human efforts such as meditation and acts of love and charity.

For Christians grace is the only way through which they may receive salvation. Jesus gave his life for us on the cross without our doing anything to deserve it. 'It was while we were still sinners that Christ died for us' (Romans 5:8). His death met the requirement of God's justice. As a result he can offer us pardon and forgiveness. All we have to do is respond in faith.

Anti-ritualism

The Gurus taught that spiritual merit could not be achieved through carrying out rituals. They rejected other practices used by Hindus and Muslims including self-mutilation, excessive generosity, fasting, meditation when not focussed on the Lord, pilgrimages, painting one's face, the sacred thread worn by Hindus, dying a heroic death in battle, and worshipping sticks and stones.

Ritualism has crept back into Sikhism in various forms but nevertheless the Sikh teaching against it parallels the Christian doctrine, mentioned above, that salvation cannot be achieved through works. A witnessing Christian can remind Sikhs who are caught up in good works that the Granth teaches the impossibility of being saved by them. This may open the door to explaining that salvation can only be found in Jesus.

God's presence

Both Sikhs and Christians believe that God may be experienced in private prayer and public worship. His presence is necessary for true worship and fellowship.

Fellowship

For Christians the true church is not a building but the community of believers, the body of Christ. Similarly the entire Sikh community is known as the Panth. Both Christians and Sikhs value fellowship with other believers and regard it as an essential element in the practice of their faith. The New Testament tells us how the early church was made up of groups of believers rather than individuals. The apostle Paul established churches wherever he went. In the 20th century Christians still receive strength and a sense of security from their membership of a local body of believers. Worship with others is an essential part of their faith. In Holy Communion they share as a family in receiving the bread and wine, the symbols of Christ's sacrifice on their behalf.

Sikhs lay similar stress on being part of a local fellowship. They reject the idea that any Sikh should detach himself from the congregation to pursue salvation on his own. The sharing of kara prasad (p. 87) and the langar (p. 37) are an essential part of Sikh practice. There is not even any special priestly class in Sikhism.

The feeling of warmth and oneness Sikhs experience while joining in community worship and the langar can be compared to the experience of Christians who worship and share together.

Suffering and Evil

Both Sikhism and Christianity regard suffering in earthly life as only part of the story. They give no rational or theological answer to the question, 'Why do people suffer?' But both encourage their followers to hang on to the conviction that God does know what is going on, and to remain faithful to him.

For Sikhs the issue is clear-cut: Guru Nanak taught that suffering is a part of life as real as joy but not as welcome. It can only be endured by obeying the will of God.

But the New Testament offers us something more hopeful than 'grin and bear it'. It sees the suffering of Jesus as a central part of God's plan. The devil is active in the world, causing trouble and pain for his own ends. But Jesus rose from the dead, demonstrating the power of love to overcome evil, sin and death. The

Christian can resist the devil in the victory of Jesus, and his hope for the future is secure in this too.

Service to Others

Both Christians and Sikhs believe that God is the parent of all human beings. They should work as his co-partners in the world caring for all people as if they were part of their own family.

Christians know the commandment in Leviticus to 'Love your neighbour as you love yourself' (Leviticus 19:18) and its illustration in the parable of the Good Samaritan (Luke 10:25-37).

The Sikh doctrine of sewa (p. 73) teaches that service to others is the greatest of all human virtues. Wherever a Sikh community is found sewa should be one of its characteristics.

Both Christians and Sikhs are taught that they should seek enough for their daily needs and give away what is surplus rather than selfishly expecting a superabundance for themselves. For both, prayer should focus on seeking God's will in their daily life rather than going their own way.

The True Guru

There are various references in the Granth to the Sat Guru (True Guru) but some uncertainty as to whom they refer. For example, 'For the Word is the True Guru and the True Guru is the Word; and through the Word one knows the Path of Emancipation' (GS 1248).

Guru Amar Das wrote, 'He who believes in the True Guru, he is saved both here and hereafter'(GS 105).

Some Christians from a Sikh background feel that the phrase the True Guru refers to God himself and that we can point to Jesus as its fulfilment. There are many parallels between the qualities ascribed to the True Guru in the Granth and those ascribed to Jesus Christ in the Bible. However there are also differences and we should not skate over these in order to make Christian teaching more acceptable to Sikhs. If we do they may feel that Sikhism has everything and they do not need Jesus.

The Granth teaches that the True Guru:-

❏ has a divine nature

❏ is creator of the world

❏ is called by God

❏ reveals the truth about God through his Word

❏ is the giver of peace

❏ is the only hope of purification from sin

❏ is the breath of life

The Bible tells us similar things about about Jesus. He:-

❏ has a divine nature

❏ is the creator of the world

❏ was sent into the world by God to save men and women from their sins (John 3:16)

❑ is the truth and provides the way to God (John 14:6).

❑ gives us peace with God

❑ is the one through whom salvation can be received (Acts 4:12).

❑ reveals God to men

❑ gives us spiritual life

However many Sikhs are not aware of the references in the Granth to the True Guru. So this is *not the place to start* in sharing about Jesus with Sikhs unless they are scholars or teachers already familiar with the references.

Despite all the common ground between Sikhs and Christians, Sikhism is powerless to save men and women. When talking with a Sikh friend you can share what you have in common but realise that emphasising this unduly may strengthen his resolve to maintain his faith because Christianity seems so close to his present beliefs.

Significant differences may have greater potential for drawing him to Christ. They may not make Christianity more appealing at the outset but the need to make a choice will be clearer. We shall deal with these differences in the next chapter (after which there is a double dose of 'things to do ').

Chapter 14

DIFFERENCES BETWEEN SIKHISM AND CHRISTIANITY

Despite the surface similarities between the two religions Sikhism and Christianity are based on very different philosophies and practised for widely differing ends. When talking with a Sikh don't begin by listing what you consider the shortcomings of Sikhism. But do get to know how his beliefs and practices influence the way he thinks about spiritual matters..

Scripture

As the Guru Granth Sahib is made up entirely of poetry it is rich in mysticism and can be interpreted differently by different people. It is more a hymn book than a statement of faith. The Bible does have some mystical passages but there is also a great deal of straightforward moral and ethical teaching, and statements about God's character and his activity in the world.

The Nature of God

Guru Nanak emphasised the oneness of God and his role as the supreme creator. He presented him as supremely a God of love. But Nanak had no place for God's wrath. Men and women, he said, should not fear God's anger but be afraid of not receiving all the benefits of his love. In contrast to Sikhism the Bible declares that God is righteous and holy. When his holy standards are violated he displays his wrath. Yet his wrath is not incompatible with his mercy and love. It is meant for the ultimate good of mankind.

In some ways the Sikh concept of God is contradictory. Whereas some statements seem to mean he is personal others state that human souls eventually merge back into God, who is an impersonal essence. The Westerner cannot resolve these apparently contradictory statements but Sikhs seem to have no difficulty in doing so. God is said by them to be both the creator and the created, the fisherman and the fish, the water and the net.

The Nature of human beings

Sikhs deny the reality of man's sinful nature. They teach that people are essentially good; the divine spark within them needs only to be fanned into a flame of goodness. On the other hand, the Bible teaches that men inherit a sinful nature from Adam; a person's guilt must be atoned for. Guru Nanak taught that a man's sins are moral lapses caused by his environment. They may be cleansed through meditation and prayer.

Uniqueness of Christ

This is the area of greatest disagreement between Sikhs and Christians. Sikhs reject the uniqueness of Christ as the only way to God. They say he is one with

Moses, Mohammed, Buddha and the Gurus, and that all paths to God are equally valid. The concept of faith in a person and the saving action of his death and resurrection are totally absent from Sikhism.

Salvation

The Gurus taught that if deliverance is sought in the proper manner all will eventually receive it. Nevertheless most Sikhs are uncertain of salvation. Grace is viewed as something which God bestows on those he chooses. A man or woman receives salvation when it is in their destiny to do so. But given enough time and rebirths all will eventually reach that point. So Sikhs believe that there is no such thing as eternal damnation; all will eventually achieve deliverance from the bondage of earthly life. Therefore ultimately no one is lost but is re-united with the divine absolute. There is no personal resurrection. The human soul is of the same essence as God, comes from God and will eventually be merged back into him. Heaven and hell are not places where individuals live for eternity but refer to different stages of a person's earthly life. In contrast Christians believe that those who receive Christ as their Saviour are adopted into God's family. After their earthly life is over they will have eternal fellowship with him in heaven. They will not lose their unique personal identity. Similarly hell is a reality where those who have rejected the Lord will spend eternity.

The Holy Spirit

Christians believe that the presence and power of the Holy Spirit is essential if a person is to live as God intends he should (Galatians 5:13-26). Sikhs believe in the presence of the divine soul within man but don't look to it as a means of helping them to live their earthly life. They have no satisfactory answer to the question of how a man can live a life that pleases God except, 'try harder'. Christianity makes impossible demands on a man or woman but at the same time indicates that the Holy Spirit is the power through whom these may be fulfilled.

The concept of the Trinity is foreign to Sikhs. However their concept of Guru, Nam and Shabad (chapter 6) could be useful in explaining it.

Good and Evil

Despite the stress on the love of God in Sikhism there is a darker side. Sikhs believe that both good and evil come from God. Though some of them think evil spirits exist they have no sense of an evil being who opposes God. Sikhs are never told to resist the devil, as a Christian is, because they do not believe in him. Evil, they believe, is the result of a person making wrong choices.

Meditation

Sikhs believe that meditation on the Granth draws them closer to God; it cleanses a person from sin and instils godly qualities in him. They see it as a means of salvation. Christians do not believe that meditation can set anyone free from sin but do value it as way of drawing closer to God, hearing his voice and discerning his will.

Sikhism cannot save

Despite all the similarities between Christianity and Sikhism the latter cannot save anyone. Its teaching falls short of God's revelation in the Bible; which makes it clear that only a personal faith in what Jesus did on the cross can qualify a person for salvation (John 1:12). Sikhs deny that God ever came to earth in the flesh and died for men's sins. They fall into the heresy of the Galatians, which was a mixture of grace, human merit and self-righteousness (Galatians 3). Some of the terms that Sikhism uses are familiar to Christians. However their content and meaning is different, so they are not adequate for salvation.

Things to do

EITHER

1. If a Sikh friend has any criticisms about Christians, listen to them. If they are the result of misunderstandings try to clear them up. If Christians were unnecessarily hurtful, apologise for them.

2. At your next meeting start to talk about beliefs you have in common. Then gently introduce those over which you differ. Be gracious about how you do this. Don't get into an argument.

3. Ask your Sikh friend to tell you what Sikhs believe about:-
   a) God's plan for mankind
   b) How one can find salvation
   c) the Holy Spirit
   Then tell him what Christians believe about these matters.

4. Set aside time to pray for your Sikh friend especially bringing to mind anything you have talked about concerning the things of God.

OR

1. If you do not yet have a Sikh friend get to know someone of that religion in the ways already suggested in this book.

2. Work out how you would explain to a Sikh the Christian truth about atonement for sins. Use simple, everyday words rather than religious terms.

3. When you next meet a Sikh friend ask her to tell you which parts of her faith are most important to her. Listen carefully to what she says and think about the things you could also accept. It will usually be acceptable for you to tell in return what is most important to you.

Chapter 15

WITNESSING TO SIKHS

Witnessing to Sikhs is more than a matter of giving appropriate literature or even of saying the right words. They will quickly sense from your behaviour whether you genuinely care for them or are only interested in making converts. Nevertheless, if you are going to witness to them effectively you need to prepare yourself. This will take time and effort but it is a small price to pay compared with what Jesus has done for us. Here are some suggestions of ways to do so.

Know the Bible

Always have a Bible with you when visiting Sikhs so that you can show them any passages to which you refer. Sikhs treat their scriptures with great reverence and expect us to do the same. So don't carry your Bible under your arm, or casually pushed into a pocket. Don't put it on the floor near your feet, in a bag on the floor or under a pile of other material. It may be best to carry it in a bag but take it out carefully when you want to use it and then put the bag down. Never use one you have marked in any way. If Sikhs are to visit your home make sure you place your Bible on the highest shelf in your sitting room, preferably covering it with a cloth. Handle it with respect. One Christian from a Sikh background suggests this can be an opportunity to talk to Sikhs about reverence for God's Word, pointing out that it is no good giving honour to the written letter and not obeying it. It is our hearts that need to be kept holy and not just a book.

Training Classes

In some areas, classes are held locally about reaching Sikhs for Christ. If they are not available in your area, why not ask your minister to organise some. You might suggest he gets in touch with *Satya Bhavan*, The South Asian Study Centre, which provides part-time courses to equip Christians for mission among Hindus and Sikhs. Trainers can come to your church on a weekly or weekend basis *(see advertisement at end of book)*.

The death of Christ

Though Sikhs do not see Christ as unique they can understand that he gave his life for others. Three of the Gurus were martyrs, as well many unknown Sikhs, who lost their lives in standing out against those who opposed their religious faith.

Sikhs are also drawn to the Christian who puts God and his fellow human beings before his own welfare. Your conduct is more important than thousands of words of preaching.

Pray

Prayer should underlie all our activity for God. Pray daily for your developing friendships with Sikhs. If you ask Christian friends to pray with you, or for you, be sure you can trust them to be absolutely discreet. Any gossip could destroy your opportunities as well as damage people you hope to lead to Christ.

Sharing your testimony

If you talk about God, Sikhs will want to know how he has worked in your life. This will impress them more than any explanation of Christian theology. You can tell them how God has guided you, answered your prayers, saved you from mistakes and changed your attitudes. But don't talk interminably about your experiences. Most people switch off when you do. Think through the really important parts of your Christian experience and practice telling it in five minutes. This will help both you and your Sikh friend to see what really matters.

Let Sikh friends tell you of their own religious experiences and stories about their Gurus. Do not denigrate them. But remember we follow Christ because he died for our sins and no Guru has ever done that. The lives of the Gurus demonstrated some aspects of God but the only person who showed us his totality is Jesus Christ.

Trust the Holy Spirit

You may use every available human means to communicate God's truth yet still feel you are not 'getting through' to a Sikh friend. Remember you are only responsible for witnessing. Convincing Sikhs that the truth is in Jesus is the Holy Spirit's responsibility.

If you find witnessing difficult ask the Holy Spirit to meet each situation in which you find yourself, guide every conversation and take you beyond your natural abilities.

On the other hand, you may be so full of enthusiasm for sharing God's truth that you want to witness to every Sikh you meet. Ask God to temper your desire with his wisdom. Not all of them will be open to consider seriously what you share, even though they may talk freely with you. Allow the Holy Spirit to help you discern those in whose hearts he is at work. Otherwise you may waste many hours with people who are not really interested.

Long-term involvement

If you are serious about wanting to win Sikhs for Christ you must be prepared to spend time building up a relationship with them. Few Sikh converts came to Christ in an instant. Their struggle to understand the new truths they were encountering probably took months, even years. Making an actual commitment to follow Jesus, with all that implied of opposition from their Sikh family and community, was not usually a matter of a moment either. You also need to discover whether an interested friend is a devoted Sikh or only a Sikh culturally. This will affect the way you share Christian truths with him.

Don't confine your friendship with an interested Sikh to purely religious activities. Enter as far you can into all that concerns him. See chapter two for suggestions about how to do this. He needs to know you genuinely care for him. In fact a demonstration of Christian love in the every day affairs of his life may be more telling than all you say about your faith.

Realise the cost of becoming a follower of Christ

A Sikh who decides to follow Jesus needs to know that Christians will be there to support him if his former friends and family disown him. He may need a place to live. It is not enough to find him a bed-sitter in some boarding house or hostel. He needs the love and warmth of a Christian family at this crisis time in his life. He will find it less of a culture shock if he can live with an Asian Christian family rather than a western one.

A young person will find marriage a problem as most marriages in a Sikh community are arranged by the family. They will usually pressurise him to marry a Sikh, hoping to bring him back to his former faith. Western Christians who know a person in this situation must put aside any preconceived ideas they may have about arranged marriages and do their best to find him a Christian partner. Several agencies, such as the Alliance of Asian Christians, would help anyone needing advice about this (p. 219). Very often, for a Sikh, becoming a Christian in the West means adapting to some extent to Western culture. We do not realise how much our culture has influenced our faith. Even young people who have grown up in Britain find it a problem. Insensitivity about this can result in them returning to their old religion. If you have the opportunity to help a Christian from a Sikh background do be sensitive to his cultural as well as his spiritual difficulties. Do not impose preconceived western standards on him. It is important to allow the Holy

Spirit to guide him about such matters as cutting his hair and discarding his turban.

Inviting a Sikh to Church

Be careful how you do this. Never invite him as an easy way out of talking to him personally about your Christian faith. Establish a real friendship in which he feels he can trust you before issuing an invitation to attend church. Christian festivals such as Christmas and Easter are the best times to do so. Sikhs have their own festivals and are often interested in ours. Whatever the function to which you invite him, remember to explain beforehand what will happen, particularly if he is coming to a service. If it is a festival tell him the story of what it celebrates. When you do invite him, do not just expect him to turn up. Arrange to meet him or call for him.

Even so misunderstandings may arise: Harbans, a Sikh, was invited to come to a 'meeting' by Ranjit, a Christian friend. Although Harbans kept saying he would come, he never did so. Eventually Ranjit asked him if he had a problem. Harbans then explained that he expected the 'meeting' to be like one he had experienced at a gurdwara where people had shouted at and insulted each other.

Despite your explanations a Sikh friend will probably still find it hard to worship in a western style. Difficulties may arise the moment you reach the church door. He is used to taking off his shoes and covering his head before entering a place of worship. When he gets inside he may be shocked to find people sitting on chairs instead of the floor. He will feel it is dishonouring to God. He may be upset too to see men and women sitting together. In the gurdwara men and women sit on opposite sides of the room. He will be particularly disturbed if young people of opposite sexes are talking freely to each other, especially if they are holding hands or expressing affection in any way. He may well feel that what is going on cannot be worship.

A Sikh may be further put off by receiving three or four unfamiliar books and embarrassed as everybody else flicks confidently through them. Books are not used for worship in the gurdwara. Many Sikhs know their hymns and prayers by heart. The rhythm and harmonies of western music may also sound strange to his ears.

After the service introduce your Sikh friend to your minister and other church members. A cup of tea at this point will help him to feel more at home. Do not, however, make a huge fuss of him. This will embarrass him and perhaps put him off coming again. Later you may be able to ask him what he thought about the service. Don't get annoyed if he criticises it but try to explain the Christian attitude to worship.

A less off-putting way of introducing him to the Christian faith would be to invite him on a church outing or to a Christian film in the church hall.

If a Sikh becomes a Christian he may at first feel more at home in a house group. Pray about the church to which you should invite a potential disciple. Different styles of worship appeal to different people. Remember that, as a Sikh, wine has been taboo, so introducing him to a church where wine is used for communion may be inappropriate.

A Sikh who is keen to learn more about the Christian faith will probably welcome the chance to do Bible study with you, either one to one or in a small group. Use the Good News translation. It is the easiest one for people from a non-Christian background to understand. The vocabulary is also simple and easily read by someone for whom English is a second language. Such people may also benefit from using one of the dyglot versions published by the Bible society. These have English on one side and the appropriate Asian language translation opposite.

Have a Genuine Concern for Sikh Friends and Acquaintances

You should not approach Sikhs merely as targets for the gospel. Nor use love simply as a tool for evangelism and leave a person to struggle with their every day problems once a 'decision' has been made. Ask God to enable you to act as Jesus did to the Samaritan woman he met at the well (John 4). He did not see her simply as a person to whom he could give his message. He showed real love and concern.

Davinder, a Sikh teenager, began to attend a church where the love of its members drew him to Christ. But once he had been baptised they thought his problems had been solved. They failed to realise they had only just begun. On hearing that he had become a Christian, his parents threw him out of the home. For many nights he slept in derelict warehouses. He asked a Christian hostel to take him in. They did so. For two nights! He only received real care when he was picked up by the police and put on probation. His probation officer, a caring person, though not a Christian, helped him to find secure accommodation and re-establish himself.

Moral Standards

In South Asia people are assumed to belong to one religious group or another. They think being British is equivalent to being a Christian and compare our present day standards of morality unfavourably with their own. But Jennifer, whose Sikh next door neighbour expressed such a thought, turned it to her advantage. She explained her neighbour's mistake and then said, "Would you like to read about the standards Jesus set?" and offered her a gospel.

Use straightforward English

Sikhs whose first language is not English know basic words and phrases but not idioms. However those brought up in this country use the same language as their peers. Always use plain English and not religious jargon.

Some Warnings

Don't pressurise a Sikh to accept Christ

Many people love to please. If a person professes faith in Christ out of politeness, it can hinder him from coming into a real relationship with Christ at a later date.

Don't be over anxious about identifying with Sikh friends

Remember no amount of language study and outward transformation can make you a Punjabi. Don't adopt Punjabi dress and lifestyle in an attempt to reach

Sikhs. They know they are a minority in Britain and may be suspicious of your reasons for trying to copy them. Western women may, however, enjoy wearing a sari or salwar kameez for a party, or other special occasion, and this is acceptable. When in a Sikh home you should, of course, avoid giving offence. Accept food they offer. Notice their behaviour and adapt your own (see chapter two) but don't go overboard about it. It may be counter-productive when you come to sharing the gospel.

Don't appear patronising

We must never imply that we feel superior because we are white or even because we are Christians. We come to Sikhs as fellow-sinners, saved by grace. Realise that shyness can be misinterpreted as aloofness. If you find it hard to talk to strangers ask the Lord to help you. He promises you the power of his Holy Spirit. Jesus said, 'Do not worry about what you are going to say.....for the words you will speak will not be yours; they will come from the Spirit of your Father speaking through you' (Matthew 10: 19-20)

Don't Run down the Sikh religion

Sikhs are proud of their heritage. Instead of telling them what is wrong with their faith emphasise the positive help you find in Christianity. *Ask a Sikh what his scriptures say. Don't tell. Remember you are not an authority on Sikhism but some one with an understanding of the Bible which you want to share with your friend. Never be disrespectful to Sikhism*

– 158 –

when talking to a Sikh. It may destroy your witness to him.

Don't be afraid to admit you don't know all the answers

When you don't know the answer to a question a Sikh asks, say you will try to find out. If you cannot do so, admit your ignorance. But share the joy and peace of trusting God for what you don't understand.

Don't get involved in philosophical discussion

Asians will talk about their religion as British people discuss the weather or different brands of soap powder. Being involved in this will usually get you nowhere as far as sharing the reality of Christ is concerned. If a Sikh friend brings up some philosophical matter try to draw him back to the basis of the gospel.

Practical Aids to Witnessing

The Bible and Scripture portions

Not many enquirers will want to receive a whole Bible but many will accept a gospel. The Bible Society publishes gospels in Gurmukhi. The Scripture Gift Mission produces selections of Scriptures for free distribution.

When a Sikh becomes a Christian he should be encouraged to read the Bible regularly, preferably morning and evening. This will help to provide him with a basic Christian foundation. If you want to give him Bible reading notes in English vet those available carefully. Some are unsuitable for a new Sikh convert

because they assume a nominal Christian understanding and some background knowledge of the
Bible. The SEAN material Abundant Life and Abundant Light may also be useful.

Other Christian literature

Asian Books, a ministry of South Asian Concern,
holds stocks of most literature suitable for Sikhs in
Britain. They are available in both Gurmukhi and
English and include tracts, stories of Sikhs who have
come to Christ and simple explanations of Christian
truths. The biography of Sadhu Sundar Singh and the
film of his life, 'Journey to the Sky' have proved
particularly useful.

Again some Christian literature is unsuitable for
people of another faith because it assumes some
previous knowledge of Christianity. Tracts or booklets talking about the new birth, eternal life and the
concept of Jesus as the Son of God will fail to make
their point without some prior explanation of these
Christian truths. Some literature stresses the beliefs
Sikhs and Christians have in common. This may
strengthen the Sikh view that Christianity and Sikhism lead to the same end. A straightforward narrative, describing the life of the Lord Jesus, is usually
the most effective way of introducing Christianity to
someone of another religion. Without some knowledge of this many Christian beliefs are hard for them
to understand.

Cassettes

These days many people do not read much. Older
Sikhs may be illiterate. The only way to reach them

is through the spoken word. Language Recordings International has a wide selection of suitable tapes. Many music tapes in Asian languages are also available through Kingsway with South Asian Concern.

Videos

Most Sikh families in Britain own a video recorder. There are a number of Christian videos suitable for evangelism. One of the most best is the 'Jesus' film in Punjabi. The 'Jesus of Nazareth' film shown on T.V. some years ago is also extremely effective in putting over the gospel. Make regular appointments with Sikh individuals or a family to watch the different parts. 'If You Sikh' is a helpful video recently produced by the Christian Video Group. As you watch these films pause to give extra explanations as needed. For an up-to-date list of available videos consult South Asian Concern.

Your local Christian bookshop may not really be able to judge what is suitable for Sikhs. You will find the organisations listed on page 219, which specialise in outreach to Asians, more in touch.

Witnessing together with others

Though personal witness is effective there are other means of evangelism which you can use with a group. If your church is in an area where there are Sikhs, encourage your minister and elders to organise some outreach activities. These can include door-to-door visiting, distributing literature and open-air services. For an open-air service the witnessing group should be multi-racial and some singing and preaching should be in Punjabi if possible. You can also run bookstalls at public events such as carnivals and shows. Some churches in Sikh areas have arranged evangelistic missions in the area with the help of an outside team. But this is only worthwhile if local Christians are willing to commit themselves to follow-up afterwards.

Most children enjoy holiday clubs and like hearing Bible stories. When the story teller relates these to the children's everyday life they can be valuable teaching tools. But do be careful not to pressurise those from Sikh families to accept Christ and go home and tell their families. At one holiday club a team member did this with a nine year old Sikh girl. She was never seen again at any Christian activity. You can help children to appreciate how much Jesus loves them and leave the suggestion of making a decision for him until they are mature enough to stand up to pressure. However you may find children taking such a step even though you have not mentioned it. If so it is vitally important that you maintain strict confidentiality.

Consider organising weekly meetings for young people and children if your church does not already have any. In an area where Sikhs live, some of their young people may join. As they experience the love and care of the leaders and hear Christian teaching they are often attracted to the person of Jesus. There may be no immediate fruit in the way of conversions. But some Christians who were formerly Sikhs tell of what these groups meant to them when they were young. One church in London has seen a number of Asian teenagers come to Christ as a result of attending regular weeknight activities as children. Sanjit made friends with Daniel, an Asian Christian boy in his club. Daniel loved Jesus and told Sanjit about him. Sanjit warmed to Daniel's friendship and openness. He also enjoyed the five minute Christian slot in the weekly club programme. After about two years he also put his faith in Christ. Never underestimate a child's ability to witness.

Some adults have found helping young people with homework a fruitful way of making friends with them. But this can take up a lot of time. Ask the Lord for guidance before committing yourself to helping an individual.

Christian women with young children have sometimes found their avenue of service in mother and toddler clubs. They invite Asian neighbours similarly placed to join them and find this a helpful way to form friendships. If it is a Christian club literature can be available. A very brief talk (two or three minutes only) and some simple choruses for the children may be included if appropriate.

You can also build on Christian festivals. At times like Christmas and Easter some Sikhs are willing to come to an explanation of the festival or a drama with music. A procession through the streets of your local area at such a time is another way of drawing people's attention to the celebration. If several churches join together for this it can make a significant impact.

Local churches may think of other ways to reach Sikhs. The possibilities for building relationships with Sikhs are only really limited by the creativity of Christians.

Things to do

1. Do a book swap with a Sikh friend. Give him a gospel or Christian biography to read and take what he offers in return. Prayerfully read this material. It will give you an insight into how Sikhs approach spiritual matters.

2. The Sikh Missionary Society gives literature without charge to those who ask for it. Write to them at the address on page 222 and they will send you a selection. Read the material prayerfully.

3. Try to find some church members who enjoy drama and practise acting a Bible story you can perform. Include former Sikhs in the cast if possible. Invite friends, especially Sikhs, to watch its presentation.

4. Pray with your Sikh friend for any special needs in his family.

5. Arrange an occasional Seeker service on such topics as our Christian responsibility for the third world, the Christian attitude to racial prejudice, or 'do all roads lead to God?' Invite a Christian speaker you know can handle effectively whatever topic you choose. Plan the programme carefully. Sloppy presentation can ruin the effect.

Chapter 16

COMMON SIKH OBJECTIONS TO CHRISTIANITY

The aim of evangelising anyone is not to persuade her to change from one religion to another but to introduce her to Jesus Christ. Inviting her to join the church or have fellowship with other Christians is inadequate and, with Sikhs, usually ineffective. Membership of her local gurdwara can give a Sikh a great measure of fellowship and security; but it cannot introduce her to Jesus. He is the only one who has atoned for anyone's sins and can offer her the certainty of eternal life.

When speaking to a Sikh about your faith, and especially when trying to counter objections to the gospel, remember that the key issues revolve around the uniqueness of Christ. Never compromise on this issue but make sure you know and can defend your belief.

If a Sikh friend asks you about your faith, para-phrase her question back to her to make sure you really know what she is asking. You may have to deal with the same issue several times and on different occasions before your friend fully grasps the meaning of what you are saying. Do so calmly and without irritation. Realise that in the end you can never lead a Sikh to Christ. Only the Holy Spirit can do that. Prayer is your most effective tool.

Sharing the Christian message with Sikhs is exciting and challenging. Do not be discouraged when difficulties and misunderstandings occur. Your friend may have previously met with undesirable behaviour from people who were apparently Christians, so that she is now prejudiced and suspicious. Do not run these people down, thus giving her the impression that Christians are divided among themselves. Speak about the positive aspects of what your faith means to you. Make sure your character and behaviour reflect Christ's love and concern for your Sikh friend even though you disagree with some of the comments she makes about Christianity. Here are some of the common reactions you will meet.

'Christianity is just another way of worshipping God'

When witnessing to a Sikh try not to give her the impression that you want to introduce her to another way of reaching God, but to God himself. He is the ultimate goal of all sincere seekers. Allow her to meet Christ and let everything else be a separate issue. Let her be 'a disciple of Christ' rather than 'a Christian'. It is all the same to us but less threatening to a Sikh.

'Jesus cannot forgive sins'

Sikhs see Jesus as simply another holy man, like their own Gurus. They were not divine but just human beings who lived close to God. No human being can forgive another's sin. You will not be able to persuade a Sikh friend that Jesus can do so. Only the Holy Spirit can do that. Many Christians from a Sikh background testify to having a personal revelation of Jesus. Sadhu Sundar Singh, one of the best known of all Sikh converts, was highly offended when Christians told him that Jesus could forgive sins. He even burned a Bible that was given to him. But one night Jesus visited him personally, in a vision, and his life was totally changed. He spent the rest of it travelling throughout the Punjab and further afield proclaiming that only Jesus could forgive sins.

'All ways lead to God'

When you first tell a Sikh that you believe Jesus is the only way to God she may accuse you of being narrow-minded, arrogant and intolerant. Arguments will not make her change her mind. Let your attitude show humble thankfulness to God that Christ revealed himself to you so that the charge of arrogance cannot stick.

Sikhs see no need for anyone to change their faith. On the contrary, they believe that people should remain in the faith in which they were born. Because of this, few Sikhs are interested in persuading outsiders to adopt Sikhism. You can explain, not that Christianity *is* a way, or the way but that *Christ said* He is the true and living way and that no one comes to God except through him (John 14:6).

Some Christians like to attend Sikh worship to see what happens, but this may give the impression to a seeker for God that it is possible to have a foot in both camps. Some Christians, like Pat Hooker, feel it is courteous and helpful to visit a gurdwara.[1] Others, often from a Sikh background, think that Christians should not even attend Sikh weddings, funerals or social activities, for fear of appearing to compromise. If you receive an invitation to attend such a gathering make it a matter of prayer. Whatever you decide, make sure you are fully committed to the Lord without reserve. Most Sikhs are discerning and respect a person who is truly dedicated to him.

'Christianity is a western religion.'

This statement again assumes that there are many valid ways of reaching God. Most Sikhs believe that Christianity is for white people and Sikhism for Punjabis. Sadly this is also the case in some parts of the Christian community. So religion is seen as a matter of birth.

In South Asia everyone is presumed to belong to some religious community or other. Children born to Sikh parents are expected to remain Sikhs and those born to Westerners, Christian. Most older Asians in Britain still hold this view.

With the exception of the Syrian church in South India, Christianity was brought to India by white missionaries. The local people assumed it was part of the white cultural heritage. Because Christian missionaries came to India when Britain ruled the country, most Indians equate Christianity with foreign domination.

In western art, Jesus is usually depicted with blonde hair, blue eyes and a white skin. This confirms South Asians in their belief that Jesus was western.

You can explain that he was born in the Middle East and that his lifestyle was Asian rather than European. You can also tell them that Christianity reached India before it came to Britain; the Syrian church in South India can be traced back to, at least, the second century A.D. Furthermore, tradition says that Thomas, the disciple of Jesus, went to South India and established the Mar Thoma church there. Tell them that today also Christianity is not confined to the west. Much of the Christian world is non-white.

'Christians are intolerant'

Some Christians seem to think that the way to witness to a Sikh is to tell her the shortcomings of the Sikh religion. This is unhelpful. Many Sikhs know more about their own faith than we ever will. Share with them the love of Jesus for all human beings and the wonder of knowing him as your Saviour. Demonstrate his love in all your relationships with Sikhs. Let them be drawn by his love and his sacrifice on the cross.

'We don't approve of the Christian lifestyle'

Some Sikhs, especially the younger generation, are attracted by certain aspects of Western culture, such as its music, customs and social activities. Others are repelled by its ideas and morals. Many from both groups mistakenly assume that everything they see in western culture is a reflection of Christianity. Older Sikhs view western behaviour with distaste. In their culture men and women do not talk to each other in public, let alone show affection for each other, even if they are husband and wife. Respectable women dress modestly. They consider the dress of many British women immodest and provocative. They are offended by the open presentation of sex in the media.

One of the first things we must do when we get to know a Sikh is to explain to her that Christianity and western culture are not one and the same thing. She will understand when you explain to her that being a Christian is not just a matter of outward behaviour, but of the inner attitude of the heart. The Granth teaches the same thing about being a Sikh. You may be able to suggest she reads the New Testament to discover the standards Jesus set. Be sure that your own conduct reflects what you say.

'Christians are racist'

Sikhs sometimes point to the prevalence of racism in British society as a condemnation of Christianity. This again illustrates their mistake in assuming that everything western is Christian. You need to explain to Sikhs that true Christians condemn racism just as they do.

'Christians take young people away from their families'

Most Christians are aware that certain cults, such as the Moonies, separate young people from their families. But some Sikhs feel deep pain and even anger when one of their young people accepts Christ. Because of the close-knit nature of the extended family, anyone who questions its activities or views, or steps out of line is labelled a traitor. When a young person starts to associate with Christians and attend their worship services her family feels threatened.

They are afraid that she will adopt western habits, take an English name and forget about the family. We should not underestimate the pain they feel at the supposed betrayal of a member.

A young Sikh who becomes a Christian may be turned out of her home and rejected by the Sikh community or shipped to India to get married. However you should encourage her to remain faithful to her family in every way she can. The love of Jesus shown in her life can overcome persecution.

One young woman who was turned out of her home because she became a Christian has worked hard at reconciliation. With the help of her sister she has been able to persuade her parents to let her visit the family home again, though so far not to live there. She goes weekly, taking with her a gift of fruit or Indian sweets or whatever else she feels appropriate. When her mother was in hospital she visited her regularly. Recently her father said, 'We are unhappy that she has left our religion. We could not keep her in the family home. But we are happy that she still seems to love us. In fact more than some of our other children.' Maybe one day he will realise that he is seeing Jesus in her.

It is difficult to win older people to Christ, especially fathers and grandfathers, but this does not mean we should not try. When someone becomes a Christian we should begin to pray regularly for the salvation of his whole family. If the head of a family becomes a Christian the rest will often follow. Group, rather than individual, decisions are part of Asian culture.

Darshan's story, in the next chapter, illustrates this well.

'What about Northern Ireland?'

If questions are raised about squabbles between Christians, make it clear to the inquirer that these are red herrings. The key point to communicate is that Christianity turns on the person and work of Christ. Disgreements between his followers are secondary.

Things to do

1. Decide what are the important parts of your testimony. Write it out so that it takes no longer than five minutes to tell. Then tell it to a Christian friend and ask for her reaction before telling it to Sikhs.

2. Hold an evangelistic prayer meeting with interested Sikhs.

3. If your church does not have gospels in South Asian languages ask your minister to obtain some (see the address list at the back of the book). Then ask a Christian friend to join you in some door to door visiting. If you cannot recognise the different languages take a selection. When someone is interested offer her several and let her select the one she reads.

Chapter 17

DARSHAN'S STORY

Born in humble circumstances in a poor Indian village - brought up working in the fields in the Punjab - I find it hard to believe how far God has brought me. Now aged 57, the mother of six, I have him to thank for the last 28 years living in England.

Having moved to England with my husband and two young children, I continued in observing my faithfulness to Sikhism - my parents' religion and their parents' before them. But I soon began to realise that going to the temple was bringing me no joy. It was as if I was only going through the motions. What grieved me most of all was that in the very place where we were supposed to be worshipping we were also backbiting and gossiping about fellow members of the Asian community.

However, at the top of the street stood a church which somehow began to attract my attention. Ten years ago, when I was to undergo an operation, I went to the temple to offer milk and to say a prayer. Yet I did not find the comfort or peace that I was looking for. Once in hospital I found that my bed looked out on to that same church, and as I lay there I saw a light shining from the church. It was at that moment that I felt something start to happen in my heart, and I was comforted.

At about this time, a nephew of mine living in the Midlands, had become a born again Christian. Soon afterwards my eldest daughter, my sister and the rest of her family turned to Christianity. They shared the good news of Jesus with me. I too wanted to believe but was afraid of what my husband would say. My niece came and explained the gospel to me in language I could understand. I knew I had sinned before God and my niece led me in a prayer of repentance. I still did not dare tell my husband that I had become a Christian. Thankfully he asked no questions when I stopped going to the temple on Sundays. I prayed for God's guidance, wondering how I was going to stand and grow in my new found faith since I can neither read nor write. It was then that my daughter phoned me in tears saying, 'Mum, according to the Bible, unless you believe on Jesus you will go to hell.' From that moment I lost my fear of man. I knew that I had eternal life in Jesus and that was more important than what people thought of me. Through the use of tapes and cassettes, I started to listen and learn about this Jesus whom I now believed in with all my heart.

Although I had stopped going to the temple, I was still invited to social events organised there. I still felt obliged to go. But one day on the very morning I was supposed to go I experienced what I now know was a vision. I saw Jesus and He told me I could no longer go to the temple because, 'Now, you belong to me'. After that I stopped going altogether.

Soon after this my sister helped me to find a local church to attend. My daughters and I would go to church together. Although initially my husband gave his permission, he soon began to dislike my going to church. He had hoped this was just a phase we were going through and that it would pass. He felt he had humoured me enough and I had to stay at home.

My 18-year-old daughter continued to go to church and expressed a desire to be baptised in water. My husband worried about what the Sikh community would say and how he was going to marry his Christian daughter into a Sikh family. I shared his anxiety until God spoke to me saying, 'Don't worry, cast your burdens on me. It's not your problem any more, it's mine.'

Daily my faith was being strengthened and I openly started to tell my Indian workmates that I was Christian. There was no turning back - everyone knew.

I would be lying if I said that my life as a Christian has been easy up to now. Sometimes it has been difficult to put my faith into practice and not bow to family pressure and the customs and traditions with which we were brought up. One instance particularly stands out. My eldest son was to be married - the traditional way because his marriage had been arranged. As part of the ceremony I was required to light incense and pay homage to our deceased relatives. At the time I knew it was wrong to bow before anyone other than Jesus, but urged by my family and caught up in the rituals of the ceremony I chose to please them rather than God. After that I experienced what I now know was a result of my sin - partial blindness.

I would be walking down the street and my eyes would involuntarily close. It got to the point where I had to take time off work. My husband took me to consult a private doctor. After checking and rechecking they just prescribed rest because they could not find the cause. But through it all I believed my Lord would heal me. I realised the root of the problem and re-pented of my sin and asked for forgiveness. I told the Lord I would never commit the same sin again when marrying off my other two sons. After three months of this condition, I experienced something that to this day makes me stand in awe of the God I worship. One day, at dawn, I was woken with a blinding light. I was healed and with a heart full of joy I went to church to sing the praises of my God and to tell of this miracle.

From the beginning my greatest enemy had been the fear of man, of what my friends and relations would say. But God dealt with me in such dramatic ways and spoke to me so clearly that I could not ignore His sovereignty. He took care of everything and gave me a close core of Asian Christian friends who under-stood my worries and sustained me in prayer. I knew that I was not alone.

My husband was my greatest critic and from the very beginning had always been so sceptical about my faith. But the Word says that you and your family shall be saved and I knew that one day he would bow the knee. Although it was tough going, I know that God knows exactly what he's doing. My husband is no longer with me but I can rejoice that only months before he died, he gave his life to Jesus and that one day we will be together again.

My family in India, my parents, my brothers, sisters and all of my husband's family were curious to know about our change in faith. As I would talk to them about Christianity and about what Jesus had done for me they would say, 'it sounds so beautiful when you talk about your guru.' I would explain that he is not a holy man or a guru, but the living God. I would share how God came down to earth and lived amongst us. I would give Bibles to those who were interested and every time I go back to India I give out the word of God in the villages. Surprisingly, none of my immediate family seemed to object to my having become a Christian. My mother was the only one to express her concern because she thought I had become Muslim, since she had heard that Muslims believed in Jesus.

Two years ago when I went to India I rejoiced to learn that my brother and some of his family had become Christians through the witness of my sister and daughter. They in turn shared the gospel with my mother who is now in her nineties. But she was adamant that she had no need to repent because she had never murdered or stolen etc. When I arrived, without any prompting from me, she expressed a desire to be 'dunked in water like you lot' - baptised in water. Unsure whether she understood the implications, a local evangelist and friend came to speak to her and heard from her that she had secretly repented and accepted Jesus and that she wanted to be baptised in water. Imagine my joy when, before my family and friends, I saw my elderly mother profess her belief in Jesus by being baptised in a tank of water in our home village. Remembering how she accused me of being a Muslim, it was so beautiful to see her find the truth and have the assured knowledge that she will live forever.

This year I saw her and in the interval she has experienced pressure from her non-believing family who find it difficult to accept her belief in an invisible God. We were able to encourage her. My daughters and I were then able to share our testimonies before a crowd of 200 or more family and friends in my husband's home village. What a privilege – some have never even heard of Jesus! God has also given me a burden for my homeland, for my family back in India. Although I cannot read or write, God has given me so much and my heart goes out to those with whom I grew up, their children and their children's children; that they would not live and die in ignorance of the gift of life that there is in Jesus Christ, the only way.

Chapter 18

DIFFICULTIES FOR NEW CHRISTIANS

Follow up

If a Sikh friend becomes a Christian do not assume he has 'arrived'. He will need a great deal of support as his struggles are probably just beginning. Explain any matters of Christian belief that are still new to him. Encourage him to talk to you about difficulties he is experiencing in being a Christian. Join him in secular activities such as sports and visits to places of interest. In short, be a real friend.

Social pressure

A Sikh may be strongly drawn to Jesus Christ but overcome by fear of how his family and/or community will react if he openly professes to be a Christian. We have already mentioned that he will be part of an extended family with its own culture, faith, heroes, history, customs, festivals etc. Deeply embedded in the life of a Sikh, probably more than in any other Asian religion, are warm relationships, affection, cooperation and a deep sense of brotherhood. To a Sikh considering Christianity, the possible loss of these can never be fully compensated for by the gains. The powerful impact of such a deterrent to conversion cannot be over stated. It is also often why Christians from a Sikh background backslide.

One young Sikh woman who was attracted to Jesus Christ said, 'To think of breaking away was something bigger than life......I believed there were only two ways a girl could move out of her father's house, in a wedding gown or in a coffin'. In the minds of many Sikhs, leaving Sikhism is more of an issue than choosing to follow Jesus. One writer suggests that a new disciple should remain in the family and work to maintain their respect and support. This would be difficult because lifestyle is linked with religion. He will find that some of the family customs in which he is expected to take part are not suitable for a Christian. 'How far should I respect my family's wishes?' is a question with which he will often struggle.

Family Honour

The family will also feel there is a stigma attached to having a Christian in their family. In the minds of many older Sikhs Christianity is associated with outcaste groups from whom most of the early Punjabi Christians came. Family izzat (p. 116) or honour and prestige in the community may be a powerful force in dissuading a Sikh enquirer from coming out openly for Christ. If he does so his family will certainly put a great deal of pressure on him to return to Sikhism; this will be emotional and occasionally physical.

The cost of becoming a Christian

Because of these difficulties it is not easy for a western Christian to know how to advise a sincere

Sikh enquirer. He must be told that there is a price to be paid for following Christ (Matthew 10:24-35). It is dishonest not to do so. He has to choose whether salvation is more important to him than peace in his family. One writer suggests appealing to the acute business sense of most Sikhs and their desire to get a good bargain. It is a bad deal to bend to social pressures in this life and be lost eternally.

How to support Asian Christians

Christian witness should not stop at delivering advice. A Sikh who professes Christ needs support to stand against the resultant social backlash. His Christian friends must realise just how much a Sikh who becomes a Christian gives up in the way of security, support and affection. The sense of belonging to one another is far stronger in Sikh families and in the Sikh community than in western ones. Westerners cannot fully understand just how much family relationships are woven into the fabric of a Sikh's life. He feels separation much more keenly. By his standards most Westerners are cold and unfriendly. The routine handshake after a service with the hope expressed that 'we will see you next week' is quite inadequate for him. Invite him to your home for a meal and make him feel he will be welcome whenever he comes. Meet him during the week not only for sharing Christian truths but just for the pleasure of each other's company. Take part together in some activity. Attendance at week-night meetings will not be what he regards as true fellowship either. One Christian from a Sikh background told a western Christian worker, 'I became a Christian from an Asian background. I lost my family. I lost the society's support around me.......and all I got in return were meetings.'

Evangelise groups rather than individuals

Because of the intense pressure experienced by individuals who become Christians it is good to aim evangelism at a larger group – at least the nuclear family. When a couple are united in their Christian faith they are much more able to withstand pressure.

Street evangelism, tract distribution etc. may bring in a few individuals but the best way to evangelise is through families and professional groups. When a Sikh comes to Christ pray regularly for his whole extended family. One person who did this found that over 20 members of such a family came to Christ.

Young Sikhs also wonder where they will find their future spouses if they openly come to Christ. Punjabi culture places a much higher priority on marriage than western culture. To remain unmarried is unthinkable. Yet the number of young Punjabi Christians from a Sikh background is small. Some Sikh converts have married a partner from a different Asian background. Some have stepped right out of their culture and married a Westerner. Because of the cultural adjustments required by both parties this can lead to some problems as the couple learn to live together.

Christian fellowship

We have already explained why it may be difficult for a new Christian from a Sikh background to appreciate Christian worship (p. 154f) Encourage him to keep on coming to church with you. If you are not always available introduce him to another church member who is; don't leave him to face this new experience alone.

Joining a house group or cell is a good way of helping him to make Christian friends. If your church does not have any other members from the same background as himself, help him to find a group of South Asian Christians meeting in your locality. If you do not know of one, do ask South Asian Concern; its address is given at end of the book. Worshipping with them sometimes will help him to feel less isolated. Some former Sikhs find it helpful to meet others who have stepped out of another faith into Christianity. If they are being persecuted by their family or former religious community or have been thrown out of their home they can talk with others who understand their situation at first hand. This is not to suggest that they form cliques. But Christians from their own cultural and religious background, who have been in similar situations, can support them in a way no one else can. This should not replace membership of a local church. The church is the only community in which new Christians can be nourished in the word of God, grow in faith and Christian understanding and eventually find security. All church members should be encouraged to help them reach this goal.

Whatever 'methods' you use in witnessing to a Sikh, remember to pray for him daily. Ask the Holy Spirit to open his heart to the truth and to enable you to share your faith with love and humility. These should characterise all you say and do.

Things to do

1. Encourage Asian Christians from a particular family group to meet regularly for worship and prayer. This should not to be a substitute for membership of a local church. Suggest they invite members of their non-Christian family to join them. The latter will usually be attracted to come to such a non-threatening gathering.

2. Work alongside Asian Christians in your area. Ask for their advice about sharing the gospel with non-Christian Asians and also how, together, you can support new Christians

3. Partner an Asian Christian in some door to door visiting.

4. Pray for Asian Christians you know.

Chapter 19

EXPLAINING THE GOSPEL

When approaching Sikhs with the gospel you do need to know something about their faith. This does not mean that you have to become a good Sikh yourself. What is crucial is that you are a well-informed Christian, walking closely with God, and open to any opportunities that the Holy Spirit gives. You should read your Bible regularly, exploring its meaning and developing your personal relationship with the Lord Jesus. Then when you share the gospel with a Sikh friend you will know instantly from feedback whether she has understood what you are trying to say. You will sense the shades of variation between the teachings of the Gurus and the truth about Jesus Christ.

However, you must be 'as cautious as snakes and as gentle as doves' (Matthew 10:16.). Sikhs look with disfavour on any person or organisation they think is trying to bring division within their ranks or extract members through conversion to another faith. Speak the truth when asked questions about your Christianity but do so in a non-threatening manner. Don't try to impress Sikh acquaintances with your knowledge of Sikhism but concentrate on aspects of your own faith which are most likely to lead to fruitful conversations. Here are some tips for doing so.

What to concentrate on

Start with similarities

Sikhism has much in common with Christianity but also things which are different. To ignore the differences may compromise your witness. At the same time it is unfair to emphasise the differences and ignore the similarities. These can form bridges by which you can gain a sympathetic hearing. In Acts chapter 17 we see that Paul did this when first speaking with the Athenians. Don't, however, spend all your time on the similarities or you may give the impression that Sikhism is just as valid a way of approaching God as Christianity (See chapters 13 and 14).

Sikhs will understand about loving God and worshipping him. They do the same. They will also agree with you that prayer is important. Quite early in your friendship with a Sikh you can ask if you may pray with her about any problems she may have.

Three of the Sikh Gurus were martyred and they therefore understand about Jesus dying for his refusal to compromise his faith and as a symbol of self denial. They are also drawn to the Christian who denies himself for the sake of others. A life which demonstrates self-sacrifice will say more than thousands of words of preaching.

Sikhs believe in the spiritual nature of human beings and talk about their faith much more readily than most English people. They also long to know God personally and will identify with what you say about your own personal experience of God.

Use the Bible

The Sikh Scriptures depict God as loving and merciful but do not show their readers how to be set free from their sins. A Christian can tell them that this loving God sent his son to break the bondage of sin and offer them eternal life.

You must make it clear that the Bible is the final authority in all matters pertaining to God. Sikhs will understand how you feel because they view their own scriptures in the same way. On the other hand it is hard for them to accept that the Bible supersedes these. Only the Holy Spirit can convince them of this. You should pray for their enlightenment.

When you have talked with a Sikh about Jesus you can offer her a gospel and ask her to study the life and claims of Jesus. John's gospel is the best one to give because its mystical approach is similar to that of the Granth. Suggest that as she reads it she should make notes of anything that puzzles her. Next time you meet you can discuss it.

Make sure you study your own Bible daily so that you can refer to it when talking to a Sikh. Here are some verses that you will find particularly helpful:

Ephesians 2:8-9   The meaning of grace

Matthew 16:16   Jesus, The Son of God

John 3:16   How to come to Jesus

1 Thess. 5:14-15   Service to fellow men

Romans 3:23	All men are basically sinful
Romans 4:24-25	Why Christ died
John 20	The resurrection
John 14:16	The Holy Spirit
John 14:6	Only one way to God

Sikhs have a great sense of history and love the stories of their Gurus. So they will appreciate your telling some of the parables and incidents in the life of Christ. These often convey the truth more effectively than abstract points.

Tell them about the Holy Spirit

A devout Sikh longs to please God. You can share the good news that after we have accepted Christ as our Saviour he does not expect us to struggle on our own to achieve the standards he sets. He gives us the Holy Spirit who provides us with the power to do so.

Avoid Christian jargon

Many of us are so used to the religious terms used among Christians that we do not realise that other faiths interpret them differently. For instance, if we talk to Sikh about being born again he will instantly think we are referring to reincarnation (p. 69). At the same time avoid borrowing Sikh religious terms hoping to express Christian truths in a way Sikhs will understand; these cannot be wholly accurate. Instead of using the word 'sins' talk about specifics such as telling lies, hurting people, thinking wrong thoughts. The phrase 'being saved' will mean nothing to a Sikh. Instead, explain the meaning of the cross, in simple language. Do not use such biblical terms as

'Messiah', 'covenant' and so on. These are meaningless to a Sikh.

In short, think through beforehand the Christian jargon you are accustomed to using. Then find ways to express what you mean in simple English instead.

Demonstrate Jesus in your daily life

Sikhs are attracted to Christ by his life of unselfish love and sacrifice. The lives of Christians who profess to be his followers should show the same virtues. 'Sewa' or 'service'(p. 73) is one of the basic doctrines of Sikhism. Devout Sikhs are outstanding in the service they render to others. A Christian who puts the welfare of others before his own will win more Sikhs to Christ than one who lives for himself. This cannot be stressed strongly enough. On the other hand do not give the impression that this is all there is to Christianity.

Tell a Sikh friend how you pray

This will show that your concern for your fellow human beings is rooted in your relationship with God. Otherwise she may think your behaviour is just a result of your trying hard to live a worthy life. When the opportunity arises, pray with her. A simply-worded, personal prayer will be more effective than a long, traditionally patterned one. She will be challenged by the personal relationship with God which it demonstrates. Be careful not to be condemning when you pray. And do not try to preach a sermon as you do so. Ask her about the needs in her family and daily life and simply bring them before the Lord.

If a Sikh with whom you are in contact seems interested in the gospel, try to get the names of her family members and their relationships and pray for them. Whole extended families have come to Christ in exactly this way.

EXPLAINING WORDS AND CONCEPTS

Sikhism is incomplete

The word 'Sikh' means a learner or disciple in active search for truth. You can build on this positive attitude. A Sikh who is a genuine seeker should be open to new insights that will move her nearer to God. That Christians have the answer may not be immediately apparent but must be communicated eventually. Focus on the reality of Jesus. Other concepts are not insignificant but should not detract from the the central issue of the person and work of Christ. Orthodox Sikhs revere God but their image of him is distorted. The solution does not lie in condemning them but in coming alongside in loving concern to explain the way of God more accurately. You can approach a genuine seeker after the truth as Philip did the Ethiopian (Acts 8) and Peter, Cornelius (Acts 10).

The origin of Life

Sikhism teaches that life is a continuous cycle of births and deaths. Only after a person has gone through this process thousands of times can he hope to be absorbed into God. Without debating the merits of a belief in reincarnation you can simply ask a Sikh, 'Have you found God yet?' Usually the answer will be in the negative. You can agree with her that God is never-ending and share the biblical account of creation. This tells us he always was and always will be. But that one day his whole creation, as we know it, will cease to exist. Then you can say that the Bible teaches that our individual lives do have a beginning and an end and that we must respond to God now, in this life.

The Christian concept of eternal life

Ask your friend what she believes will happen to her after death. She will probably be uncertain. Explain what Jesus offers. Tell the story of the resurrection and show your friend that this assures us of the hope of living with God in heaven. We don't merge into him like a drop in the ocean but enjoy life forever as his children. This explanation is crucial. One of the attractions of Christ to a Sikh is that he offers *a clear hope after death*.

The second Coming of Christ

This Christian belief has no parallel in Sikhism. Orthodox Sikhs believe that the Gurus were messengers of God but not divine. God, they say, would no more put all things under them than under any other member of the human race. The reality of the kingdom of God in the heart of Christians now, and over the whole world at the second coming, is not a Sikh concept. When you speak about this, show her some of the many places in the Bible where this is mentioned. There are over three hundred of them in the New Testament. They include John 14:3 and Matthew 24:30-31. You may need to go over this teaching several times with a Sikh friend as it will be

such a new concept to her. In the end only the Holy
Spirit can convince her of the truth, so prayer will be
your best weapon.

The meaning of sin

Sikhs will understand when you talk about the
emptiness of life without God, the sense of guilt and
the longings for peace which accompany it. Many of
them have experienced such feelings. Do not tell them
in a superior manner that you have the answer. Come
alongside them in love and concern and share times
when you have felt the same way.

Sikhs believe that sin is something which affects
them from the outside. Human beings are attracted to
people and things in this world; to their own self-in-
terests instead of focussing on God. Other evils in the
human character stem from this. Sin is the performing
of an unworthy act, with the stress on action. Share
with them sensitively that sin comes from our own
hearts and is the result of our disobedience to God.
The concept that sin came into the the world through
the disobedience of one man will be hard for them to
grasp. We sin because we are sinners; the evil in the
human character stems from this not from some outside influence. The question of what to do about their
own personal sin has troubled men and women
throughout the ages. Do not go on to tell them that
Jesus is the answer until you have established the fact
that they are in need of salvation from their own
personal sin.

Salvation from sin is found only in Jesus

Sikhs do accept that men and women have a problem with sin and that they need to do something about it. You can say that the Bible likewise tells us this. But man alone *cannot change himself.* You could tell the story of the rich young ruler (Matthew 6:24). Jesus Christ came to help us change.

When your Sikh friend recognises her need of forgiveness you can tell her how you found the answer in Jesus. Sikhs are familiar with sacrifice, personal suffering and martyrdom. To tell your friend about the crucifixion of Jesus will not necessarily make a big impression. Sikh history has many martyrs. You must explain that Jesus' death was unique. He died for human sin, whereas Sikh martyrs died for their relig-ion. Jesus died once, in order to bring us to God (Hebrews 10:1-18, 1 Peter 3:18). God cannot merely overlook sin because this would mean violating his own justice. Only Jesus' death made forgiveness pos-sible.

You can point out that while the Sikh Gurus did many admirable things they provided no means of forgiveness and no way to change. You can ask your Sikh friend how the stories of the Gurus can effec-tively make an individual a better person today. Tell her Jesus is alive today and miracles still happen in his name.

The doctrine of karma, that the consequences of one's sin are reaped when one is born again in another body, is a part of Sikh teaching. The truth that Jesus took the karma of the whole world, on the cross, is revolutionary teaching for a Sikh. The idea of bearing one's own punishment for one's sins is deeply embedded in Sikh belief.

Sometimes a Sikh will ask, 'If forgiveness is so cheap won't people easily commit the same sin again?' You need to explain how God helps us not to sin again and that loving him means choosing not to sin.

You may have to explain the Christian concept of sin and forgiveness, through the cross, many times before the truth sinks in. In the end only the Holy Spirit can open a person's understanding. Pray earnestly for Him to do so. It is a wonderful moment when a Sikh realises that she is free from the necessity to pay for her own sins.

Jesus, giver of peace

Most Sikhs long for genuine peace in their hearts. The search for it permeates their religious experience. But few will say they have found it. Telling them of the peace you have as a Christian may be a way of introducing them to Jesus. You can use such verses as John 14:27

Jesus, giver of love

Many Sikhs, when open and honest, will acknowledge that there are tensions in their homes and among different groups in the gurdwara. And a sincere Christian will have to admit that this is true in some Christian homes and churches too. But she can live her personal life in a way that honours Jesus and demonstrates the difference he makes in producing true love among his followers.

Jesus, the fulfilment of the Granth Sahib

Many statements in the Granth, the expectations of its authors, and the evidence of their longing for God are fulfilled in Jesus.

Jesus is unique

Even though a Sikh may agree that Jesus is a very special person who offers salvation to all who come to him, he will probably object to your saying that he is the only way to God. The Gurus taught that there are many valid routes to Him. When a Sikh does declare her faith in Jesus, make sure she understands that this means forsaking all other ways and following only him. She must realise that Jesus cannot be just another painting on the wall alongside Guru Nanak and Guru Gobind Singh. Failure to deal with the tendency to compromise the uniqueness of Christ will have long term implications. Make sure a Sikh who comes to Christ is fully assured that he is the one perfect incarnation of the creator God.

The doctrine of the Trinity

If a Sikh has heard about this she will probably ask you if you believe in three Gods. You should be prepared to admit that Christians have difficulty in grasping fully the mystery of the three in one and one in three. It is one of the deeper things that Christians spend their life searching into, and grasping it is certainly not a precondition of opening one's heart to Jesus.

If a Sikh asks you any questions you cannot answer, admit it. But say you will try to find out. Consult your minister or an experienced Christian about what to say before you meet that person again.

Some Practical Approaches

The keys to reaching a Sikh for Christ are prayer, patience and perseverance. You probably learned the details of your faith over many years. Therefore, do not expect a Sikh to understand them in one or two meetings. She may never before have opened a Bible, let alone know anything about its teaching.

You need to build up a relationship of trust before you can expect her to give you her confidence or consider seriously what you say about your faith. Maybe you will not say a great deal about it in your first few meetings. You will concentrate on making friends. But as you do so she will be noticing your behaviour and forming her opinion of what Christians are like. You must stay close to God, day by day, so that what you say and do demonstrates the difference Christ has made in your life and glorifies God.

Here are some methods of sharing the gospel which you may be able to use.

The Bible and Scripture portions

In Isaiah 55:11 we read, '.......the word that I speak - it will not fail to do what I plan for it; it will do everything I send it to do.' You cannot overestimate the power of God's word to speak to the hearts of men and women. Carry a small copy of the Bible with you wherever you go, remembering the advice on page 149 about how to show respect for it. Then you can show Sikh friends any passage to which you refer.

But God's word does not depend on your presence to do its work; it is powerful in itself. God will speak to the heart of anyone who reads it with a sincere desire to know the truth. Pray for any Sikh to whom you have given a scripture portion.

Other Christian literature

Many Sikhs will be happy to read books about Christianity. They particularly enjoy biographies. Do read beforehand any book you give to them.

The spoken word

Though many Sikhs are well educated there are some women and older men for whom reading, even in their own language is difficult. But you can use the spoken language effectively. After all, many of the Bible narratives were passed down by word of mouth from one generation to another, before they were written down. You can teach God's truth through music, drama, poetry, videos, paintings, visual objects etc. Sikh friends will often accept invitations to events which include these before they are ready to come to a church service.

Public meetings

Do not invite Sikh friends to Christian evangelistic events until you have built up a relationship of trust with them. Explain beforehand what is likely to happen. If a speaker invites people to go forward to receive Christ don't try to persuade your friend to do so. If she goes of her own free will, pray for her as she is being counselled. And pray that the counsellor to whom she is allotted will be sensitive. Never use any sort of pressure tactics on her. Calls to raise hands, go forward or sign decision cards are not wrong in themselves but if a person is pushed into a decision for which she is not ready it may do more harm than good. It is better to leave a Sikh to make her own decisions.

The use of testimonies

Sikh friends will be interested to know how you came to faith in Christ. It may be the first time they realise that being born in a Christian family or country does not make a person a Christian. Each individual has to make his own personal decision. Conversion stories of other Sikhs who have come to Christ may be helpful. But the terms of the gospel must be patiently and repeatedly explained if a Sikh is to come to a real faith. If a former Sikh is giving his testimony or if it appears in an evangelistic magazine or tract be careful how you use it. Some Sikhs are suspicious of this, viewing it as propaganda. A one-to-one discussion where questions can be asked and answered is likely to be more fruitful.

Baptism

Prior to his baptism a Sikh who associates with Christians may be seen by his family as merely socialising. But afterwards they will view him as having deserted the Sikh cause and become a Christian. They will usually also think he has become a Westerner, will adopt a western name and lifestyle and reject his family. Baptism is a major turning point in the life of a former Sikh. His family will usually feel he has betrayed them. The next chapter will deal with some of the results of his action.

Things to do

1. Obtain some cassettes of Asian Christian music and lend them to a Sikh friend. When she has listened to them ask her what she thought of them.

2. Think through what are the key facts of the Christian faith. Write them down so that you can share them with an interested Sikh. This should not take more than five minutes to tell.

3. Learn the Bible verses suggested in this chapter. Try to use some of them the next time you talk with a Sikh friend about your faith.

4. Find out the names of family members closest to your friend and pray for them regularly.

Chapter 20

RAJ AND REBECCA'S STORY

R_{aj} writes:

I was born in west London and grew up in Southall where I attended the gurdwara with my mother and grandmother. I received basic instruction about Sikhism from them. But as I read English translations of books on Sikhism I found many of life's questions remained unanswered. 'What happens after death?' was the most prominent one. And 'Who is the one and only true God?' From an early age I felt uneasy when I thought about death or heard it talked about. So I tended to avoid it and put it to the back of my mind.

Three events took place in my life which frightened me and led me to search for God. In all of them I had a close call with death and my fear of it came to the forefront. The first was when I lost my balance and fell backwards at over 1,000 feet on a mountain in South Wales. However a friend caught me in time. The second was at the firework festival of Diwali when a large rocket, descending from above, narrowly missed my head. The third time was when I was 17. I had practised martial arts for ten years and was very self confident, feeling I could face up to any attack on my person. However, one day two thugs ambushed me in an alley and held me at knifepoint. I was taken by surprise and could do nothing to defend myself. I was fearful for my life. Eventually they released me unharmed. As a result I became disenchanted with martial arts and life. I began to search for God and answers to my questions.

One day I picked up a New Testament, which had been given to me at school. I turned to John chapter 14 and read, 'Peace I give to you, my peace I leave with you. I do not give as the world gives. Do not let your heart be troubled and do not be afraid.' Whilst reading that I felt a deep sense of peace unlike anything I had previously experienced. At that point I knew that if I accepted Jesus into my life and continued to read the holy Bible all my questions would be answered and my fear removed. A few days later, on December 23rd 1986, I found a church near home, went to it and asked Jesus to come into my life and be my Lord and Saviour. I asked him to forgive me for all my sins. I was 18 years old at the time. Since then my life has changed in many good ways. I have found real joy, peace and happiness and also solutions to life's problems. I know that I'm forgiven.

Since becoming a Christian I remember climbing a mountain in Cumbria. At a height of over 2,000 feet I stepped on some ice and almost fell off the edge. But at no point was I afraid. I trusted God and knew that he was with me. Had I died that day I know for sure that I would have gone straight to heaven to be with Jesus.

My wife Rebecca's testimony is different. She was brought up as a nominal Asian Christian. But she did not practise her faith or live like a Christian. Born in Pakistan she came to the U.K. at the age of 13. Until she entered college her experience of Christianity was traditional. She had no experience of the freedom there is in Christ. In her mind religion was boring and irrelevant.

We met at college during which time I became a Christian. Shortly after leaving we were married. Rebecca saw the commitment I had made to Jesus and began to meet Christian couples and friends at a local church. She was drawn to these people. Their lifestyle was unique. They seemed to be enjoying the Christian life and were full of peace and joy. She saw that they were different from the Christians she had met as she was growing up. These people referred to themselves as being born again. They actually lived out what they believed and didn't just call themselves Christians by name. The commitment and love that these new friends had for God and one another really touched her heart. She began to realise that it was possible to have a personal relationship with God. She did not want to continue living an empty, ungodly lifestyle so she developed a desire to be born again and to please God. In 1988 she made a conscious decision to ask Jesus to be Lord of her life and live the Christian life according to the Bible and not human tradition. As a result, her life has been transformed over the years. The Lord has healed many emotional scars that she had been carrying since childhood. He has lifted her inner spirit and freed her from years of spiritual oppression by the evil one.

Our marriage has been strengthened as we live together with our eyes on Jesus.

Chapter 21

THE GOSPEL FROM SIKH VIEWPOINTS

Sikhs who become Christians are attracted to Jesus in various ways. If you find a Sikh friend drawn to him and his work for some some particular reason make sure you understand it yourself so that you can talk about it together. Here are some reasons that deserve attention.

God's plan of salvation

Intellectual Sikhs appreciate the Bible's clear presentation of the way to salvation. Some come to Christ by reading the Bible on their own. One student, who had a deep hunger for God in his heart, tells how he studied many religions, always praying first that God would show him the truth. One day he began to read a Bible. He had completed only a page or two when his heart began to burn within him. As he read on he realised that at last he had found the truth. He says, 'After a lot of prayer, study, and with great pain and anguish, I gave up Sikhism and accepted Christ as my personal Saviour'. His brother also became convinced of the Bible's truth. Together they studied what it had to say about baptism. Their convictions led them to take baptism and confess their new found faith to their family and friends.

Conviction of sin

Some Sikhs are convicted when they read or hear that all men are sinners. They are aware of their shortcomings and how they affect their karma, understanding that they must suffer for them. If you are in touch with an interested Sikh make sure they know that their sins cut them off from God. Then go on to demonstrate that Christ paid the penalty for them in full and they are free. One former Sikh says, 'As I read tears flooded my eyes. I read on and was impelled to surrender my life to Christ.'

What happens after death

Sikhs are uncertain of what will happen to them after death. How will their karma affect them in their next life? Have they been good enough to ensure they will be born higher up the scale? One Sikh enquirer said that when the truth dawned on him, that after this life was over he would be with God for ever, he felt stunned by the wonder of such good news.

The peace of God

The uncertainty about how God views their sins and what will happen when they die causes a lot of anxiety for many Sikhs. The search for peace permeates their religious experience, but few indicate they have found it. The testimony of those who have come to Christ is that he gives peace. For the first time in their lives they have assurance that God is not only a judge but also a God of mercy. He also gives peace in all the details of life. One former Sikh said, 'So many things in life can shatter your peace. Now I have God's peace for my help and support I am a different person'.

The love of God

Many Sikhs long to experience genuine love. Despite the strong sense of family among them few will say they have found a love which has no strings attached. Reading in the gospels of the love and gentleness of Jesus has brought some of them to Him.

We can also show them that Jesus points to God as 'the Father'. It assures them that God cares for them as an individual. Being able to talk to Him at any time, about everyday matters, means a great deal to most Christians from a Sikh background. They also experience Him as the best sort of father who always keeps his promises.

Jesus, the Eternal Guru

Sikhs believe that the best way to come close to God is to follow the teachings of the Gurus even though they were only human beings. They also look for the Sat Guru, the eternal Guru, who will be sinless. Some Sikhs have realised that Jesus is the fulfilment of the promise of the Sat Guru, and have surrendered their lives to him on that basis.

Jesus, the Word of God

We have mentioned in chapters five and six that Sikhs believe that God resides in his Word, the Guru Granth Sahib. They speak of this as Shabad. Some former Sikhs came to Jesus by reading John's gospel, especially chapter one, where they found the statement, 'Before the world was created, the Word already existed; he was with God, and he was the same as God.' (John 1:1). When they were shown that the Word is Jesus, and that he is the Shabad, they were eager to read the rest of the gospel. As they did so they understood the unique character of Jesus, and surrendered to him as Saviour and Lord.

An encounter with Jesus

Some Christians from a Sikh background tell of having a supernatural meeting with Jesus, usually in the form of a vision. Sadhu Sundar Singh was one of them. He was so weary with searching for the truth that one night he begged God to reveal himself before dawn. If he did not do so he decided he would go down to the railway line and throw himself in front of the 5 a.m. train. To his amazement, Jesus appeared to him in physical form and assured him that he was the truth. Sadhu Sundar Singh was changed for ever. He witnessed to everyone he met and walked all over north India and into Tibet to share the gospel.

Things to do

1. Ask a Sikh friend to tell you what he finds most attractive about the Christian message. Then share with him what is most attractive to you.

2. Try to find out if there are Christians from a Sikh background in your area. If they are finding it hard to stand for Christ against Sikh relatives and friends give them all the encouragement and practical support you can.

3. Have a role-play session with a Christian friend to explore the uniqueness of Christ. Let one defend the idea and the other challenge it. After the first attempt change sides so that each has a chance to try both presenting gospel and exploring Sikh reactions.

Chapter 22

TARA'S STORY

Tara is someone who was drawn to Jesus when she realised his love for her.

My earliest memory of seeking a relationship with God is from the age of eight/nine years old. I did my Sikh prayers, particularly the japi ji sahib and attended the gurdwara every Sunday. But I continued to feel empty and thirsty for the reality of a God I could communicate with, in every day language, about emotions, instead of the pointless chanting of the same prayers without understanding them.

At the age of 13/14 years I met Linda who came from a Hindu background but who had become a Christian as a result of her mother's vision of Jesus whilst on her deathbed. Linda introduced me to the Living God. The more she told me of the personality and character of Jesus and her relationship with Him the more I realised that He was the God I had been seeking. Salvation - which I had no concept of before, was to me the icing on the cake.

Knowing that my parents would not accept my change of faith and allow me to go to church I did not tell them. So fellowship consisted of letters and rare meetings with Linda and a few Christian friends. I also found Bible reading notes helpful. Sadly, a year or so after we left school, Linda had to leave home due to pressures on her to have an arranged marriage. However God provided marvellously by opening up doors for people to visit me at home, which my parents somehow did not seek any explanation for.

Then when I was 20 years old the issue of marriage arose. This led to my confession of my faith change. Naively I told my mother I never wanted to get married and she thought this meant I was wanting to become a nun. My parents panicked and arranged my marriage rather than wait further. I contemplated leaving home but Linda's negative experiences and my own lack of a strong foundation of teaching prevented me doing this.

I got married and fell in love with my husband and ashamedly fell into the trap of believing that all paths lead to God. However 15 months later my husband died from a brain haemorrhage and my world fell apart. Initially I did not want to live, and death had a morbid fascination for me. Once more I began to search for something to fill the void and hurt in me.

My mother encouraged me to attend the gurdwara to find peace, but again I became disillusioned. My grieving process then took me through anger at God and then denying that He existed. Meanwhile my friend Linda had renewed contact with me and had herself returned to the Lord. She continued to encourage me and talk to me about Jesus but I stubbornly refused to believe. Then my nephew suffered a fit and went into a coma. Something inside me knew Jesus was the only one who could answer. Not feeling able to handle another loss through death, I called out to the Lord to save. Arriving at the hospital I found a Bible and opened it and God spoke very clearly that my nephew would live. So I returned to my faith.

I knew that my parents would still not allow me to attend church and so once more I returned to fellowship and contact with just my friend Linda. The Lord opened up many doors and provided opportunities for fellowship and teaching to strengthen my faith. This helped me to stand firm against all further offers of marriage. My parents, despite the pressures placed upon them by the community and family, accepted my decision not to remarry until God provided me with a Christian husband.

Although it has at times been difficult, 11 years on, I look back and can see that God kept me and made provision for me in many ways. He blessed me with a successful career in social work, and my own house in 1991. This meant I could attend church and even have housegroup meetings in the house.

The last two years have been the most eventful in terms of blessings and witness of God's greatness and faithfulness. The Lord has provided me with a loving husband and we now have a two month old baby son. The marriage has been a powerful witness to both our families and the community. We were able to testify to God's almightiness and his overwhelming desire to provide us with the best.

Recently I heard a song, based on Psalm 63 and Isaiah 43 and 54, which for me brought together all God's promises over the years. It is called *Mourning into Dancing* by Tommy Walker.

He's turned my mourning into dancing again
He's lifted my sorrow and I can't stay silent
I must sing for his joy has come.
Where there was only hurt
He gave his healing hand
Where there once was only pain
He brought comfort like a friend
I feel the sweetness of His love
piercing my darkness
I see the bright and morning sun
as it ushers in His joyful gladness.

GLOSSARY

akhand path	uninterrupted reading of entire Guru Granth Sahib
amrit	sugar crystals dissolved in water
amritdhari	Sikhs who wear the five Ks
Anand	Hymn of Bliss
Ardas	congregational prayer said at every service
bhakti	way of loving devotion
chunni	scarf
chaur	fly whisk waved over the Guru Granth Sahib
Dasam Granth	writings of Guru Gobind Singh
giani	scholar of Punjabi language and literature
granthi	person who looks after the gurdwara
gurbani	poetry of the Guru Granth Sahib
Gurmukhi	Sikh language
Gurpurb	festival for a Guru's birthday
guru	religious teacher or sometimes used for God
gutka	small Sikh hymn book
janam sakhi	story of Guru Nanak's life
Jap	opening verses of the Dasam Granth
Japji	Sikh morning prayer

kacha	shorts
kangha	small comb
kara	steel bracelet
karah prasad	special food distributed at end of service
karma	works
Kaur	princess, title of female Sikh
kes or kesh	uncut hair
Khalsa	community of initiated Sikhs
khanda	double-edged sword
kirpan	sword
kirtan	singing of hymns
kirtan sohilla	last prayer at night and at funerals
langar	communal free dining room
lavan	wedding hymn
manji sahib	cushion on which the Guru Granth Sahib rests
maya	attachment to the world
moksha	salvation
mool mantra	Guru Nanak's first poetic words
nam	character of God; nam simran is meditation
nishan	Sikh symbol, nishan sahib is the Sikh flag
Panj Pyare	the five beloved ones
Panth	entire Sikh community
rag	hymn

rumal	small square of cloth covering top knot
rumala	cloth covering the Guru Granth Sahib
sabha	society
sahajdhari	Sikhs who do not wear the 5Ks
sahaj path	broken reading of entire Guru Granth Sahib
Sahib	Lord
samsara	reincarnation
sangat	local Sikh community
Sat sri akal	God is eternal (greeting on meeting)
sewa	service to others
shabad	word of God
Singh	lion, title of male Sikh
soder rahiras	evening prayer
vak lao	daily advice from Guru Granth Sahib
Waheguru	wonderful Lord

Notes

Preface

1. Paul Weller (Editor), *Religions in the UK*, University of Derby, 1993, p. 524

Introduction

1. Paul Weller (Editor), *Religions in the UK*, University of Derby, 1993, p. 524

2. Ibid

Chapter 4

1. Margaret Wardell and Ram Gidoomal, *Chapatis for Tea*, Highland 1994 p. 93

2. Ibid p. 52

Chapter 6

1. Margaret Wardell and Ram Gidoomal, *Chapatis for Tea*, Highland 1994

2. Piara Singh Sambhi, *Sikhism*

Chapter 11

1. John Bowker, *Worlds of Faith*, B.B.C. 1983

Chapter 12

1. Arthur Helwig, *Sikhs in Britain*, OUP, New Delhi 1986

2. ibid

3. ibid

4. ibid

Chapter 16

1. Pat Hooker, *His Other Sheep*, Grove Books, Nottingham, 1989, p.17

USEFUL ADDRESSES

Alliance of Asian Christians, Carrs Lane Church
Centre, Birmingham B4 7SX

Asian Books, 34 Gilbey Rd, Tooting Broadway,
London SW17 10PS
(also c/o South Asian Concern)

Asian Christian Outreach, 114 St Mary Street,
Southampton, Hants SO1 1PF

Association of Christian Teachers, 2 Romeland
Hill, St. Albans, Herts AL3 4ET

Bible Society, Stonehill Green, Westlea, Swindon,
Wilts SN5 7DG

Christian Vision Group, 1st House, Sutton Street,
Birmingham B1 1PE

Church Missionary Society, 157 Waterloo Road,
London SE1 8VV

Commission for Racial Equality, Elliot House,10-
12 Allington Street, London SW1

Crosslinks, 251 Lewisham Way, London SE4 1X

Evangelical Christians for Racial Justice, 269 Rol-
tol Park Road, Birmingham B16 0LD

Home Office, (Immigration and Nationality Department),Lunar House, Wellesley Road, Croydon,
Surrey CR9 2BY

In Contact Ministries, St. Andrew's Road, Plaistow,
London E13 8QD

Indian High Commission, India House, Aldwych, London WC2

INTERSERVE, 325 Kennington Road, London SE11 4QH

Jesus Film Project, 30012 Ivy Glen Drive, Suite 200, Laguna Niguel, CA 26277, U.S.A.

Joint Council for the Welfare of Immigrants, 115 Old Stret, London, EC1

Language Recordings International, Unit 20, Moorlands Trading Estate, Bristol Road, Gloucester GL1 5RS

Oldham Resources Centre, Faith to Faith, The Salt Cellar, PO Box 14, Oldham OL1 3WW

Qalam Projects, 10 Grosvener Road, Hounslow, Middlesex, TW3 3ER

St. Andrew's Bookshop, St. Andrew's Road, Plaistow, London E13 8QD

Scripture Gift Mission, Radstock House, 3 Eccleston Street, London SW1W 9LZ

SIM(UK), Ullswater Crescent, Coulsdon, Surrey CR5 2HR

South Asian Concern, PO Box 43, Sutton, Surrey SM2 5WL

The Council of Churches for Britain and Ireland's Committee for Relations with People of Other Faiths, 2 Eaton Gate, London, SW1W 9BL

BOOK LIST

Baabra, Davinder, *Visiting a Sikh Temple*, Lutterworth, Cambridge 1988

Bowker John, *Worlds of Faith*, BBC London 1983

Cole Owen and Piara Singh Sambhi, *Sikhism*
"   "   *Sikhism and Christianity,*
                    Macmillan, London, 1993

Cole, W. Owen, *A Popular Dictionary of Sikhism*
"   *The Sikhs: Their Religious beliefs and Practices*
"   *A Sikh Family in Britain*
"   *Thinking about Sikhism,*

    Lutterworth Educational, Guildford and London

Dhanjal Beryl, *Dictionaries of World religions*, s.v. Sikhism, Batsford London 1987

Dodhia H.K. *Crossing the Cultures*, Grove Books Ltd, Bramcote, Notts 1990

Duggal K. S. *The Sikh People Yesterday and Today,* UBS Publishers' Distributors Ltd, New Delhi, India, 1994,

Fearon M. and Gidoomal R. *Karma 'n' Chips, the New Age of Asian Spirituality*, Wimbledon 1994

Farncombe Anne, *Our Sikh Friends*

Fraser George S. *The Sacred Writings of the Sikhs,* revised, George Allen and Unwin

Hooker Pat, *His Other Sheep*, Grove Books Ltd, Bramcote, Notts 1989

Loehlin C. H. *The Christian Approach to the Sikh,*
Edinburgh House Press, London, 1966
"   *The Sikhs and their Scriptures,*
Lucknow Publishing House

Lyle, Sean, *Pavan is a Sikh*, A & C Black, 1983

McLeod W.H. *Textual Sources for the Study of
Sikhism,* Lucknow, India, 1964
"   *The Way of the Sikh*

Minority Rights Group (report), *The Sikhs*

O'Connel, *Sikh History and Religion in the 20th
century*

Sambhi, Piara Singh, *Understanding your Sikh
Neighbour,* Lutterworth Educational,
Guildford and London 1986
"   *World Religions, Sikhism,* Stanley
Thornes & Hulton, 1989
"   *Meeting a Sikh family in Britain,*
A & C Black, London 1983

Raj Santosh, *Understanding the Sikhs and their
religion,* Kindred Press, Winnipeg, Manitoba, Canada, 1991

Sikh Missionary Society, {*large variety of booklets*}, 10 Featherstone Road, Southall, Middx
UB2 5AN

Thompson, Phyllis, *Sadhu Sundar Singh,* O.M. Publishing, Sevenoaks, 1994

Tully, Mark   *No Full Stops in India,*Penguin, 1992

People involved in the British Asian scene are living in a complex cultural situation.

Some are leaders of small churches or fellowship groups, needing guidelines for ministry. Others are professionals looking for an Asian perspective on their Christian faith as it relates to work and ministry.

All face tensions between multiple identities - South Asian, British, followers of Christ, many from different religious backgrounds...

SATYA BHAVAN ("the House of Truth") is a ministry of South Asian Concern. Its aim is to equip and mobilise Christ's followers for mission.

We offer
INFORMATION AND RESOURCES for cultural understanding, service and outreach

TRAINING for individuals, churches and groups:
- EAST+WEST / ASIAN EQUIP is a flexible training programme to help your group to share good news with your Asian neighbours
- THROUGH ASIAN EYES is an open learning course on ministry and mission from an Asian perspective

SATYA BHAVAN

Training, Research & Outreach to South Asians
in the UK, South Asia and the Diaspora.

SOUTH ASIAN
CONCERN

PO Box 43, SUTTON, Surrey SM2 5WL * Tel 0181 770 9717 * Fax: 0181 770 9747
Satya Bhavan is a ministry of South Asian Concern. Registered Charity No: 1002270

By the same authors

Chapatis
for Tea

Reaching your Hindu Neighbour

If you enjoyed this book, you will not want to miss its companion volume Chapatis for Tea, and in particular the first chapter entitled "A Christian response to those of other faiths".

Apart from its own interest, your witness to Sikhs will be all the more informed if you can communicate that you are aware of the differences between Sikhs and Hindus!

"As a handbook for cross-cultural evangelism, this little volume has rarely been bettered"
        from the foreword by Clive Calver

ISBN 1 897913 07 9   180pp   £4.99